RESURRECTION JUDGEMENT AND THE HEREAFTER

LESSONS ON ISLAMIC DOCTRINE

(BOOK THREE)

SAYYID MUJTABA MUSAVI LARI

TRANSLATED BY:
HAMID ALGAR

RESURRECTION
JUDGEMENT
AND THE
HEREAFTER

LESSONS ON
ISLAMIC DOCTRINE
(BOOK THREE)

SAYYID MUJTABA MUSAVI LARI

TRANSLATED BY:
HAMID ALGAR

RESURRECTION
JUDGEMENT
AND THE
HEREAFTER

LESSONS ON
ISLAMIC DOCTRINE
(BOOK THREE)

SAYYID MUJTABA MUSAVI LARI

TRANSLATED BY:
HAMID ALGAR

Jacket Design by: F. Farhang   May 2002

May 2002

Musavi Lari, Mujtaba, 1935 -Resurrection Judgement
and Hereafter:
Lessons on Islamic Doctrine (book three)/ Mujtaba
Musavi Lari Translated by Hamid Algar.- [S.l: s.n],
2002.
251 p.
Cataloging based on CIP information.

1.Eschatalagy. 2.Imamite Shiites - Doctrines.
I.Algar, Hamid, 1940 - , tr. II.Title.
III., Title: Lessons on Islamic Doctrine.
BP222 .M87.04952   297.44
                                     M78-27721

Contents

About the Author

Sayyid Mujtabā Mūsawī Lārī is the son of the late Āyatullāh Sayyid 'Alī Asghar Lārī, one of the great religious scholars and social personalities of Iran. His grandfather was the late Āyatullāh Ḥājj Sayyid 'Abdu 'l-Ḥusayn Lārī, who fought for freedom in the Constitutional Revolution. In the course of his lengthy struggles against the tyrannical government of the time, he attempted to establish an Islamic government and succeeded in doing so for a short time in Lārestān.

Sayyid Mujtabā Mūsawī Lārī was born in 1314/1935 in the city of Lār where he completed his primary education and his preliminary Islamic studies. In 1332/1953, he departed for Qum to continue his study of the Islamic sciences, studying under the professors and teachers of the religious institution, including the main authorities in jurisprudence (*marāji'*).

In 1341/1962, he became a collaborator of *Maktab-i-Islām*, a religious and scientific journal, writing a series of articles on Islamic ethics. These articles were later collected into a book published under the title *A Review on the Ethical and Psychological Problems*. Twelve editions of the Persian original of this book have been published, and it has also been translated into Arabic, Bengali, Urdu, Swahili, French, and English, under the title, *Youth and Morals*.

In 1342/1963, he travelled to Germany for medical treatment, and returning to Iran after a stay of several months, he wrote a book called *Western Civilization Through Muslim Eyes*. The book includes a comparative discussion of Western and Islamic civilization, and in it, the author seeks to prove, by way of a comprehensive, reasoned, and exact comparison, the superiority of the comprehensive and multi-dimensional civilization of Islam to that of the West. This book has recently been reprinted for the seventh time. In 1349/1970, it was translated into English by a British Orientalist, F. G. Goulding, and it aroused much attention in Europe. Articles concerning the book appeared in several Western periodicals, ånd the BBC arranged an interview with the translator in which the reasons for translating the book and the reception accorded it in England were discussed. The English version of the book has up to now been printed three times in England, eight times in Iran, and twice in America.

About three years after the publication of the English translation, Rudolf Singler, a German university professor, translated it into German, and the version he produced proved influential in Germany. One of the leaders of the Social Democratic Party informed the translator in a letter that the book had left a profound impression upon him, causing him to change his views of Islam, and that he would recommend the book to his friends. The German translation has now been reprinted three times.

The English and German versions of the book were reprinted by the Ministry of Islamic Guidance for wide distribution abroad through the Ministry of Foreign Affairs and the Islamic Students' Associations abroad.

At the same time that the first printing of the German translation was published, an Indian Muslim scholar by the name of Mawlānā Rawshan 'Alī translated it into Urdu for distribution in India and Pakistan. This Urdu translation has now been reprinted five times.

This book has also been translated into Japanese, Spanish, Arabic and French languages.

Sayyid Mujtabā Mūsawī Lārī has also written a pamphlet on *tawḥīd* (divine unity), which was translated in England under the title, *Knowing God*, and published several times in America. It has also been translated into Spanish, Russian,

Polish and Urdu languages.

In 1343/1964, he established a charitable organization in Lār with the purposes of propagating Islam, teaching Islam to rural youth, and helping the needy. This organization remained active until 1346/1967. Its main accomplishments were the dispatch of students of the religious sciences to the countryside to teach Islam to children and young people; providing thousands of school children with clothing, books and writing equipment; building a number of mosques, schools, and clinics in towns and villages; and the provision of miscellaneous services.

Sayyid Mujtabā Mūsawī Lārī pursued his interest in Islamic ethics, writing new articles on the subject. In 1353/ 1974, a collection of these articles, revised and supplemented, appeared in book form under the title, *The Role of Ethics in Human Development*. The book has now been reprinted six times, and the English translation is underway.

In 1357/1978, he travelled to America at the invitation of an Islamic organization in that country. He then went to England and France and after returning to Iran began writing a series of articles on Islamic ideology for the magazine *Soroush*. These articles were later collected in a four-volume book on the fundamental beliefs of Islam (*tawḥīd*, divine justice, prophethood, imamate, and resurrection) under the title *The Foundations of Islamic Doctrine*.

This four-volume work has been translated into Arabic, some parts of it having already been printed three times. The English translation of the third volume of this work forms the present book; the remaining volume is being translated to be published soon. Urdu, Hindi and French translations are also underway; two volumes of the French translation have already appeared.

In 1359/1980, Sayyid Mujtabā Lārī established an organization in Qum called Office for the Diffusion of Islamic Culture Abroad, later renamed, Foundation of Islamic Cultural Propagation in the World. It dispatches free copies of his **translated works** to interested persons throughout the world. It has also undertaken the printing of a Qur'ān for free distribution among Muslim individuals, institutions and religious schools in Africa, and distributes English, French and Spanish translations of the Qur'ān.

In the Name of God, Most Gracious, Most Merciful

Lesson One
The Two Aspects of Death

Although the phenomenon of life counts as the most precious of gifts and its loss is extremely grievous and terrifying, none can doubt that just as surely as man embarks on his life involuntarily to spend some time in this guesthouse we call the world, he must ultimately confront the painful and frowning face of death when the scroll of his life is rolled up.

Our world is a world of turmoil and instability. The wheel of birth and death keeps constantly turning; do not believe that anything can come into being in the sphere of this cycle without being subject to change.

Whatever comes into existence must traverse a path leading to death; it makes no difference whether it be man or one of the other countless forms of life. Every phenomenon the limits of whose motion are set by matter is ephemeral, for it is precisely its defining characteristic that draws it on toward non-existence; the end of its affair is disappearance. The funeral dirge of finiteness resounds throughout the world of being.

We must first raise the complex question of the end of life, attempt to analyse it and to answer some of the questions that may be raised in this respect.

Is life restricted to this present terrestrial existence which stretches from the moment of birth to the moment of death? Is it confined to the brief interval during which those who have come to this world take, one after another, the place of those who have left it? Should it be imagined that there is no existence other than the three-dimensional existence of this world, and that our individual characteristics and personalities bear the imprint of non-being? Or is it true that beyond this existence an eternal morrow awaits man, which will enable him to perceive anew himself and the world? Will the physical system of this world be transformed into another world and manifest a new and perfected form?

Finally, in all these arrivals and departures, in these assumptions of form and annihilations, is there some divine purpose at work? In other words, did God's will determine that man, the choice part of His creation, should live in this world as a traveller, a transient, and move ultimately to another world which will be his eternal abode?

If we conceive of death in the light of the first set of possibilities, then life — under whatever circumstances it is spent — will be full of misery and pain, for the anticipation of annihilation and non-being inevitably arouses dread in man and paralyses him with the undeniable torment it induces.

The second vantage point is that of a person who finds refuge in the concept of a world beyond nature which enables him to place this world in perspective. He is convinced that man and the universe advance together in a pattern determined by God's unity and that their forward movement is unending. For such a person death is simply the breaking of the narrow and confining cage of the body and his being liberated from it, entering thereby an ideal and enrapturing realm. For such a person death is merely the substitution of one form to another, a change of outer garb. When death arrives man abandons this garb and his form of clay and puts on the garment of the transitional realm. Then, ascending from that stage to the next and flying toward infinity, he casts off in turn the garb of the transitional realm and puts on the raiment of eternity.

For those who hold this exalted and precious belief, the end of life is a transformation overflowing with good, a transformation that enables all things to recover their identity and to be purified.

Dr. Carrel the well-known scholar says:

"The answer given by religion to the anxiety man feels when confronted with the mystery of death is infinitely more satisfactory than that given by science; religion gives man the answer his heart desires."[1]

The bitterness and unpleasantness of leaving this world are seen as natural and inevitable by those who imagine that their passage through the wall of death spells an end to all dimensions of their existence and that there is no life beyond that frontier. But for those who believe that this world is nothing more than an elaborate game, similar to that in which children or artists engage, and that quitting this world of matter is a form of progress and ascent in the direction of infinity, the matter takes on a quite different aspect. Not only does the countenance of death lose for them its horror and awe; they even long impatiently for release from their body of clay in order to be joined in union with Him.

Such an understanding of the nature of death impels man to pursue pure and exalted aims, to the point of heroically sacrificing his life for their sake. Then, like a moth freed from its prison he circles over his former place of confinement; like a warrior on the field of battle he accepts a bloody death. He sacrifices his personal motives and desires in order to attain a morrow filled with pride, glory, and lofty and positive ideals.

In the view of such a person, man has a two- dimensional life as an attribute that is uniquely his. One of the two dimensions is his material life, in which he is subject to biological circumstances and social necessities, and the other is his inner and spiritual life, a life in which he engages in thought, inventiveness, creativity, and the cultivation of ideals, gives external existence to his inner ferment and enthusiasm, and moulds to his will the society in which he lives and even history.

Fear of Death

Lack of awareness and the failure to comprehend

adequately the nature of death induce fear, dread and insecurity in man, for they make death appear to be a terrible nightmare.

Imām al-Hādī, upon whom be peace, once went to visit one of his companions who had fallen sick. The fear of death had robbed him of all tranquillity and calm, so the Imām addressed him as follows:

"O servant of God, you fear death because you do not understand it correctly. Tell me: if your body were soiled with dirt so that you were pained and discomforted and afflicted with running sores, and you knew that a washing in the bathhouse would rid you of all that filth and pain, would you not wish to avail yourself of the bathhouse to cleanse yourself of the dirt? Or would you be reluctant to do so and prefer to remain in your polluted state?"

The sick man replied: "O descendant of the Messenger of God! I would definitely prefer to wash myself and become clean."

To this the Imām responded: "Know, then, that death is exactly like the bathhouse. It represents your last chance to rid yourself of your sins and to purify yourself of evil. If death embraces you now, there can be no doubt that you will be freed of all sorrow and pain and attain everlasting happiness and joy."

Hearing these words of the Imām, the sick man changed completely and a remarkable tranquillity appeared on his face. Then in dignified fashion, he surrendered himself to death, in the shroud he had drawn around himself, full of hope in God's mercy. He closed his eyes which had now seen the truth and hastened to his eternal abode."[2]

The Master of the Godfearing, upon whom be peace, was one of those rare human beings who had truly understood the meaning of life and had caused death itself to fear him. Few men have advanced the claim that 'Alī made: "I swear by God that the son of Abū Tālib is more at ease with death than a suckling infant with the breast of its mother." The whole of his life turns out on examination to be a proof for this claim. Why should that extraordinarily pure man, who never exaggerated concerning his love for God, not long day and night for the meeting with God Almighty, for hastening to His supreme presence? With his pure nature and exalted mind he had understood that death means liberation from the dark fetters of matter and the opening of the gates of eternity; why then should he fear death?

History does not record a noble hero other than the son of Abū Ṭālib whose hand wielded the sword for almost fifty years and who encountered without spilling a single drop of blood unjustly, countless incidents which normally arouse feelings of hate and vengeance in man and rob him of his humanity.

This was his concept of life:

"Even if I were to be given the whole world and all it contains, I would not unjustly remove the husk of a single grain from the mouth of an ant."

For this pious and strong commander who throughout his life granted the weak and the powerful their rights in equal measure, who showed care for the feeding of his murderer while suffering the pain of his fatal wounds, warfare and struggle represented a means for reform of man, not his destruction.

The vile murderer calculated that he would be able to carry out the assassination of 'Alī, upon whom be peace, only when he was standing in worship before his Lord, with the whole of his being effaced in the splendor of the Creator; it was this that enabled him to implement his plan.

When he was struck with the wound that severed the cord of his life, 'Alī bade death welcome like a dear one he had long been awaiting, and said:

"I am free, by the Lord of the Ka'ba! I have no fear if death should carry me off or death should befall me."

The relatives and companions who gathered round the bed of 'Alī had never seen the same amazing tranquillity that they now saw in that ocean of courage, generosity, justice and piety, as he endured the painful wound that had been inflicted on him.

It may furthermore be said that the one who denies life after death looks on man from only one vantage point: he imagines him to be a creature wandering in the realm of matter and supposes that all of his existence is exhausted by the few passing moments his earthly body spends in this world. Such a view of things implies that the entire destiny of man consists of helpless exposure to a whole range of factors, known and unknown: he enters this world with great pain, maintains himself in it for a few days by enduring all kinds of oppression and injustice, and then finally departs in the embrace of death and annihilation.

Such a life would indeed be miserable, and to remain in the world under such circumstances would be painful. Whoever reaches this distressing conclusion about the destiny of man must view the nature of existence itself in the same way. For in his opinion it is not only whose life is spent in the whirlpool of pointlessness and injustice; whatever comes into existence must also traverse the path of meaninglessness and oppression until the moment of its annihilation. All things are engaged in injustice: whether it be man in his struggle for survival, an insect that inflicts a sting, or the drops of a rainstorm that destructively beat down on a hut. To take matters still further, this would mean that this transitory world lacks all legitimacy, that it is simply an assemblage of absurdity and injustice.

This is the view of the person who has severed his link with the eternal and everlasting being that is the source of all existence, and who thereby commits an error for which he must pay the price.

With such a person, sickness, deprivation, the inability to fulfil wishes and attain goals (or the loss of them after attaining them), fear of a dark and unknown future – all these serve to break his spirit and torment him.

* * * * *

Victor Hugo says:
"If man thinks that he is faced with annihilation, that

absolute non-being awaits him after this life, life itself will have absolutely no meaning for him. That which makes the life of man pleasant and enjoyable, makes his labor joyful, gives warmth to his heart, and broadens the horizons of his vision, is none other than what revelation and religion give man — belief in an eternal world, faith in the immortality of man, the conviction that 'You, O man, are not destined to non-being; you are greater than this world, which is nothing more than a small and impermanent nesting-place for you, a cradle for your infancy — the era of your splendor and greatness still lies ahead.'"

The feeling of pointlessness, the lack of belief in the occurrence of resurrection and reckoning after this earthly existence, has become a source of crushing fear for man in this age of the progress of science and technology. With the strong inclination to material life that results from the one-sided development of man's capacities, he has now come to regard it as his ultimate goal.

All the innovations that are meant to protect man from so many dangers and errors, to liberate him from fetters and restrictions, have in fact robbed him of peace and tranquillity and cast him into the whirlpool of anxiety. Our world has become a stage on which men rush madly forward in a single direction, for the sake of prosperity and power which they have made the source of their happiness and the aim of their strivings.

The result of this constricted view of things, the belief that the world has no owner, that man wanders through these ruins accountable to no one, is that the world is filled with fear and rapine. The smell of blood rises up from every corner of this abode of terror. This is the state of affairs that man has now reached; he is no longer himself, but a being filled with greed, cupidity, hatred and envy. It is unclear how matters will proceed. The emergence of new schools of philosophy is in itself a sign of the painful predicament in which man finds himself and of the intellectual and spiritual vacuum.

A psychiatrist writes:

"Two thirds of the patients that have come to me from all over the world are educated and successful people who are tormented by a great pain – the feeling that life is pointless, meaningless, and incomprehensible. The reason is that as a result of technology, the stagnation of beliefs, shortsightedness and prejudice, twentieth century man has become irreligious. In bewilderment he searches for his soul, but he will have no peace until he rediscovers religion. Lack of religion is the cause for the emptiness and meaninglessness of life."[3]

Evil deeds form another reason for fearing death; it is obvious that they make death appear extremely fearsome and terrifying to the wrongdoer.

As Mawlānā Jalāl ad-Dīn Rūmī says:

O you who attempt to flee death in your fear,
It is yourself that you fear – use your intelligence!
It is your countenance that is ugly, not the visage of death;
Your soul is a tree on which death is the leaf.

Yes, it is the fear of one's deeds that causes men to stand in terror of death. In this connection, the Qur'ān remarks concerning the Jews:

"*Say: 'O Jews, if you imagine that you alone are the friends of God, to the exclusion of all others, then desire death for yourselves, if you speak truly.' But they will never desire death, on account of the deeds they have freely performed. God is well aware of the deeds of the wrongdoers*" (62:6-8).

The Noble Qur'ān depicts for us the fruitlessness of the lives of those who turn their back on the truth and struggle helplessly in the whirlpool of meaninglessness: "*Those whom they invoke other than the Creator can create nothing; rather they are themselves created. They are dead and lifeless, lacking all feeling and awareness, and they do not know when they will be resurrected*" (16:20-21).

"*O Messenger, you cannot make these people whose hearts are dead hear through the word of truth, nor can you convey your summons to these deniers who avert their faces*" (30:52).

By contrast, the Qur'ān calls living and immortal those

who are killed while seeking to elevate God's word: "*Do not call dead those who are killed in God's path; they are living in the presence of their God receiving sustenance from Him, although you do not perceive it*" (2:154).

Lesson Two
Two Views Concerning
the Pleasures of This World

Man can construct a solid barrier against the danger of the dissolution of his inward personality only when he attains religious belief and certainty, the conviction that our sorrows and joys do not go to waste, that we are not advancing to annihilation, but are rather moving towards Him. In other words, our residence in this abode of clay is temporary, lasting only until the appointed day when the summons of resurrection arouses us from our tombs and transfers us from our narrow earthly abode to our eternal residence, in order to enjoy everlasting existence in the proximity of the favor, blessings and mercy of God, the infinite source of all grace.

Belief in the existence of an eternal essence bestows nobility and value on man; it enables him to become a creature that is endowed with wisdom and aspires to ascend. Without the presence of man thus defined, nature itself would become meaningless, for all of its wonders. Once equipped with such a belief, man obtains the peace of mind and tranquillity he desires.

A European thinker writes:

"When the human mind is purified and cleansed of all the evils and lusts that plague the soul, it will turn away from purely human concerns to contemplating the beauty of nature. It will take pleasure in observing the variety of animals, plants and minerals, with the different forms, qualities and substances that each possesses, together with the relationships, contradictions and hierarchies of causation that exist in every natural phenomenon.

"When man's mind advances beyond this stage, he will next begin to fly in the heavens on the wings of thought and awareness. He will gaze on the splendor, beauty and power of the heavenly bodies, witness their motion and phases, and listen to the pleasing harmony that prevails throughout the universe. A pleasure of the purest kind will suffuse his being, and an ardent desire stirs within him to discover the primary cause and creator of this masterpiece of beauty. When he becomes aware that the essence, power, intelligence and goodness of this primary cause are infinite and beyond his perception, his mind will finally have attained rest."[4]

If the world be regarded as a laboratory and the hereafter as a continuation of the life of this world, albeit on a higher plane, and the body be considered as a means of implementation or expression for the wishes and intentions of man, the personality of man is no longer restricted to a single orbit. A vast space is opened before him for his flight and ascent, and life takes on its true meaning.

The Effectiveness of Faith

If we examine the influence of belief in the hereafter in preserving social security and preventing the spread of corruption, crime and the violation of law, we reach the conclusion that this belief is the only force capable of taming the rebellious desires of the soul. It is like a protective shield that guards man from the assault of his passions, for the one who holds this belief will obey a series of ethical principles without hypocrisy and without being subject to external pressure; he will accept the discipline they inculcate with a clear conscience.

Such an aim cannot be assured simply by a high standard of education or economic prosperity, the power of technology, or by the existence of highly developed punitive mechanisms. A society that relies on these will be unable to advance toward a balanced and ideal situation.

Today we witness a growing wave of corruption, injustice and cruelty in countries which are well-developed with respect to education, economic prosperity, and judicial organization. Such is the extent of the moral decay in those countries that the forces of law and order — well organized though they are and provided with all the equipment that the scientific and technological revolutions have bestowed on them — are unable to take the place of the basic element of faith in taming the rebellious inclination of the soul to deviance and sin.

There are many people today who lament and are distressed by the present condition of their societies, but they are unable to do anything effective or to sketch out a plan of action.

A society that has fallen prey to a sick culture cannot fail to be replete with all kinds of impurity and abomination. What we mean by a "sick culture" is pessimism, the absence of goals, a belief that life lacks all meaning. Intellectual confusion is also one of the chief symptoms of a sick culture. The solutions that are proposed for the solution of the crisis are fruitless and ineffective when it comes to controlling the deviant tendencies rampant in society.

Modern science has expelled man from certain spheres of thought he used to inhabit; this is a phenomenon which has inevitably affected the whole of humanity. Insofar as man retains a firm and correct belief, this is a positive development, but insofar as he is ignorant and lacking in belief it is harmful. Man is not always in a position to draw logical conclusions from his knowledge, and if scientific civilization is to be a civilization that benefits man, true faith and wisdom must be added to man's augmented body of knowledge.

In this world where the need for the cultivation of virtue is always keenly felt, the moral capacities and abilities of men are always tested by the goods that come into their possession. It is belief in the hereafter that enlarges the inner capacities of man through a profound and qualitative transformation; they begin to unfold like an unending succession of waves. Belief in the hereafter tames the obstinacy of the self and its mad greed for the untrammelled enjoyment of the goods of this world; it brings under control all of his faculties and properties. Hoping for great rewards and fearing severe chastisement, man shuns the greedy, irrational and undisciplined accumulation of worldly goods.

For he knows that here he is dwelling in a temporary realm; his residence on earth is like that of passing caravan. When he quits his bodily form, which was simply the expression of his transitory life, and is freed from this narrow realm, the gateway to another world is opened before him, and bounties are placed before him that bear no relation to the enjoyments of this world.

Man's heart never ceases to desire as long as he is in this world. Nonetheless, belief in the hereafter will permit him to realize that the opportunities afforded by this world are limited, that the gain to be had from it is very slight, that even the portion which lies within reach cannot be retained for ever, and that delight and pleasure are not restricted to our brief days here on earth. He will not be overcome every instant, then, by an endless surge of desire, causing him to form countless attachments and ultimately to lose himself, nor will he be excessively troubled if he does not acquire an excessive amount of the bounties of this world and the pleasures they yield.

His attitude to material enjoyments will never be the same as that of the hasty person who is in a state of constant anxiety and agitation lest his possessions not last him until death. It is only for those who worship this world that material possessions count as a goal in themselves; those who are advancing towards the abode of eternity use the bounties of this world as a means for attaining lofty goal. Moreover, indifference to what this narrow world contains causes man to enjoy the inner peace that he seeks. Such peace will undoubtedly permit him to enjoy to a heightened degree those pleasures of life that are in conformity with the criteria of religion.

Rousseau says:

"I know that I am destined to die; why, then, should I create attachments for myself in this world? In a world where all things are changing and passing, where I myself will soon become non-existent, of what use to me are attachments? Emile, my son, if I lose you, what will be left for me? I must nonetheless prepare myself for such an intolerable eventuality, because no one can assure me that I will die before you.

"So if you wish to live happily and rationally, attach your heart only to beauties that are imperishable; try to limit your desires and hold duty in higher esteem than all else. Seek only those things that do not violate the law of morality, and accustom yourself to losing things without distress. Accept nothing, unless your conscience permits you. If you do all of this, you will surely be happy, and not become overattached to anything on earth."[5]

When the spirit of man overflows with faith in God and is assured of its own immortality, it will feel a remarkable and ever-increasing power within itself. Once it frees itself of absolute attachment to the perishable values of this world, it will in fact be the master of the universe.

The elevating tranquillity that results from such an orientation of the spirit gives man the ability to resist firmly the allurements of the world and the demands of the passionate self. He no longer laments the deficiencies and misfortunes that assail him, nor does he become proud and arrogant on account of his successes. Whatever causes other men to lose their bearings has no undesirable effect on him.

Belief in the day of reckoning and in the existence of an absolute perfection whose scrutinizing gaze encompasses all things and before whom the deeds of all man are present, even if they be as inconsequential as an atom – this belief creates a powerful influence in the depths of man's being that no other force can equal. Belief in God and His commands not only prevents man from fearing the difficulties of life but also transforms those difficulties into means of development and ascent toward the lofty goals of life.

Thus the Qur'ān says: "*Whosoever believes and reforms himself shall never be prey to fear or to sadness*" (6:48).

"*God shall guide to the path of happiness those who believe and do good deeds*" (10:9).

Who can underestimate the role of the spirit and the heart in the development of man and not ascribe to the heart the greatest share in the ascent of the spirit to the highest degree of perfection? Have not love and faith made possible throughout human history the greatest acts of devotion and self-sacrifice?

It is the purpose of the Qur'ān firmly to implant awareness in the inner being and heart of man, to transform his heart and fashion him in such a way that he is inwardly impelled to perform deeds of value.

Since the believer depends for success in his striving on the infinite power of God, in Whom he places all his hope and reliance, the passing hardships and sorrows he encounters will never be able to darken his life, however difficult the path to his goal may appear. He will even accept failure with equanimity, if that failure occurs on the path leading to God, and regard failure as being a kind of victory in itself.

Whoever chooses God as His protector and guardian will escape the darkness of bewilderment and misguidance.

The Qur'ān says: "*God is the Guardian and Protector of those who believe; He brings them forth from darkness into light*" (2:257).

Those who refuse to worship God find themselves prostrating before their inner idol; passion and desire rule every dimension of their beings.

Self-worship is a dangerous sickness that with its different manifestations in the individual and social life of man entails the most tragic misfortunes and disorders. It creates a powerful barrier between man and the truth and results in the breakdown of man's capacities of perception and the blinding of his inner being.

The Qur'ān says: "*Do you see the one who takes his own desires as his god? God has made him go astray, despite his possession of knowledge; He has placed a seal on his ears and his heart and drawn a curtain of darkness over his eyes. Who other than God can guide him? Will you then not take heed?* (45:23).

Since Islam regards this world as the tillage of the hereafter, it is acceptable that man should regard it as a means. Through choosing the correct path and acting virtuously man is in fact preparing his own life in the hereafter. But if man regards the world not as a passage leading to a higher, eternal life but as an aim and goal in itself, his meaningless attachment will deprive him of happiness and prevent him from growing towards perfection.

The Qur'ān declares:

"Are you content with the life of the world in exchange for the hereafter, although the life of this world is as nothing when compared with the hereafter?" (9:38).

A Unique Advantage

A unique and valuable advantage enjoyed by the one who accepts the principle of an afterlife as part of his belief system is that he knows his future is fundamentally dependent on his own conduct and deeds. His behavior is therefore based on truthfulness and the absence of hypocrisy, on purity and sincerity. Belief in the hereafter not only raises qualitatively the level of his deeds but even accelerates their quantitative growth. The richer the content of his belief, the greater will be the extent of his sincerity, to the extent that even the least of his acts will be suffused by the purest intention.

He will be aware that all of his acts are constantly subject to the severest scrutiny. Whatever good or evil act he performs will be entered in the ledger of his deeds and retained for accounting. The day will come when his account will be examined with the greatest of care, for there is no mystery that is hidden to the one who watches over him.

By contrast, one whose inner being is empty of belief in the Last Day and who denies the most fruitful of realities, imagines that he will not be called to account for any aspect of his deeds, that he will not be burned by the flames of the fire that he kindles today, and that he will not suffer the grave consequences of his corrupt deeds. He is accordingly engulfed in waves of delusion and untruth; he looks with hot desire on all forms of corruption and gazes coldly and listlessly on virtues and lofty qualities of the soul. Because of his mode of thought, if he occasionally undertakes some useful and creditable deed, this will remain unappreciated by the blind and purposeless future in which he believes. He therefore regards himself as justified in remaining indifferent to all considerations of virtue and emotion and in disdaining all lofty human qualities. If he commits various forms of crime, treachery and oppression, he recognizes no sanction other than the conventions and regulations of society that would call him to account for his misdeeds and punish him.

The fundamental shortcomings of human laws are that they assume all forms of human life will come to an end with death and that they are based on the wishes and sentiments of the majority of the members of society. Divine legislation follows a different path, one based on the eternity of human life, a life that is not severed by the blade of death, and it draws up its agenda accordingly.

A question calling for analysis is why science and the human mind are incapable of enlarging their sphere to aid in building the loftier dimensions of man and in bringing about profound transformations within him as does the fertile power of religion. The reason for the descent of man into the depths of banality and for the existence of all kinds of shortcoming in society is to be found in the very essence of man-made laws and their lack of congruence with the essential nature of man.

The religious man willingly implements the laws that the has come to accept as expressions of the eternal wisdom of God. He recognizes, moreover, that while obeying those laws he is journeying towards eternity and an imperishable realm across a span of infinite time. The narrow vision of human knowledge is incapable of fully comprehending the lofty destiny of such a man.

Lesson Three
Resurrection, a Manifestation of God's Far-reaching Wisdom

There can be no doubt that the volitional acts and motions of man, in all their variety, proceed from inner motivations. All our strivings in their different aspects, are reflections of our intentions and ideals, as well as being attempts to fulfil them; they are like so many affirmative responses to the summons of our inclinations and wishes.

Even if we imagine that some of our volitional and deliberate acts completely free of personal motivation, we must not overlook the fact that none of our modes of behavior is ultimately separable from a hidden and unspoken goal. In the depths of every act a secret and apparently unknown aim is concealed.

For example, when we conceive the intention of doing good to someone, we are not inspired exclusively by a humanitarian desire or a generous impulse, contrary to what we imagine. It is the desire for our own peace of mind which is our primary motivation.

The same is the case with any natural factor within the realm of nature; it, too, cannot lack an ideal and goal. The difference is that what man undertakes as a result of knowledge and awareness arises in nature as the product of a natural factor, totally unconnected to knowledge and perception. In both cases, then, the essence of the matter is the same; the presence of an aim and a goal.

The intellect that is free of illusion understands that the whole structure of the universe has the implicit wish to nurture within it a being that will be endowed with thought, capable of development, empowered over its own destiny, and able to emerge from the confines of subjection to the instincts, to move in the orbit of guidance by the light of its own intelligence, and to choose freely the path of ascent or that of decline.

* * * * *

In addition, science presents to us the picture of a well-ordered universe that is regulated by precise and unfailing laws and norms. It is a universe in which all things — the wing of a moth, the leaf of a tree, a grain of sand — follow precise systems peculiar to themselves and regulating their motions with geometric precision. From the atom to the galaxy which contains several suns within itself, from the galaxy to infinite space which in turn contains numerous galaxies within itself, the whole infinitude of being, ranging from the smallest particle to the largest of heavenly bodies — everything moves in accordance with a unique and amazing regularity.

This being the case, it is quite incompatible with man's intelligence as well as with his scientific thought to assert that in all the extensive — indeed infinite — activities that take place in the world there is no connection between the doer and the deed or the doer and his purpose.

Once we assume that the wondrous system of the universe has been created by an infinite knowledge and power, we cannot believe that the Creator should place in the very heart of the universe and all its creatures, whether animate or inanimate, laws that regulate their functioning, and equip each of those creatures with the means necessary for subsistence, without pursuing a definite goal in all this planning and ordering.

A society composed of believers in the unity of God, recognizing Him to possess all forms of perfection, also accept without equivocation that the order of the world has a purpose.

How can one simultaneously bear witness to the infinite

knowledge and the eternal power and wisdom of the Creator and deny that all the activity of that sublime being has an ultimate goal?

It is inconceivable that we should assert that the seed of purpose has been sown in the smallest of our bodily organs and on the other hand claim that the destination of man as a totality is emptiness and aimlessness.

Beginning with the moment that his sperm is formed, man cannot be conceived of as a being that is left to its own devices, to follow the various stages of growth simply in accordance with natural instinct. It is also not sufficient if out of all the concerns that are necessary for him he contents himself only with assuring the means of existence.

* * * * *

Generally speaking, the summons of all divine religions are based on the responsibility and accountability of man. The prophets and messengers of God have always declared, in the categorical manner that is peculiar to them, that in the vast, indeed infinite, world which lies before man, all of his deeds are subject to an accounting. Accordingly, they have emphatically exhorted those who have accepted their message to prepare themselves for the great event which will take place throughout creation, causing it to enter a new stage, be submitted to a new order and take on a new life. They have further commanded their followers to make use of their potentialities for growth, development and change in order to let all dimensions of their existence flourish and to prosper and attain salvation. They have warned them against doing anything which would earn them misery and wretchedness in the hereafter and cause them to burn in the fire of eternal regret.

With his own hand, man sows in this life the seed of his life in the hereafter; he determines himself the fate that will be his in the next world. To express it differently, his eternal life is formed from the materials he himself provides in advance.

Imagine a skilful painter who spends a great deal of time

in creating a true work of art and then destroys it. Is it possible to regard such a person as rationally sound? There can be no doubt that no intelligent person would do such a thing.

Can the purpose behind the creation of the vast and magnificent scheme of being, woven together with such consummate skill, or the creation of man with all his restless faculties and powers, be the restricted, confined life of this world, with all the contradictions it contains? Is it the destiny of man to struggle hopelessly in a whirlpool of fantasy and blind imaginings, to be the captive of false criteria of his own fashioning, and then to be scattered like a handful of dust particles in the infinitude of space once death closes the book on his life?

If this were to be the case, would it not make the Creator resemble that hypothetical artist, nihilistic and purposeless? Would it not be quite incompatible with the knowledge and wise power of that aware and creative Being the light of whose far-reaching purposiveness is manifest in the inner and outer aspect of every atom of creation?

Were the divine wisdom to be thus drastically reduced, it could no longer be a broad river irrigating the whole plain of existence.

The caravan of being is bound, in the course of its journeying towards perfection, ultimately to reach absolute perfection, and we, too, whose source of being is God, will also return to that ultimate truth.

In the general order of the universe the coming of resurrection has a certain natural inevitability. Just as darkness brings light and justice emerges from oppression and unjustice, so too the life of this world is succeeded by resurrection. If we deny this truth, we are in effect belittling the exact and precisely calculated ordinances that rule over creation, as well as the vast expanse of nature and the world which is too infinite and complex for our thought and vision to encompass. In addition, we are forgetting the principle of advance towards perfection that can be deduced from the careful observation of creation and the motion of all parts of the universe.

How can we accept on the one hand that this principle prevails over the entire system of creation, from the smallest particles of the atom to the huge and awe-inspiring heavenly bodies, and suppose on the other hand that the final result of the operation of this principle will be obliteration and utter non- being?

If this be our concept of the order of the universe, it will be incompatible with infinitude of creation and the countless phenomena that it contains. Wisdom and intelligence will be unable to reconcile with the wisdom of God, that infinite essence, the great planner of creation, the choice of this transient, material life as an ultimate goal.

Apart from the relative and transitional goals that can be observed throughout the system of the universe, there is a point of termination for all things, which the Qur'ān describes as eternity and everlasting life.

"Whatever exists in the heavens and on the earth belongs to God, and to Him is the return of all things" (3:109).

"Whatever exists in the heavens and on the earth belongs to God, and to Him do all affairs revert and return" (42:53).

The Maker has created the sublime order of being with limitless power and wisdom; He has brought into being countless creatures throughout the expanse of the world; and from among them He has chosen man as the supreme product of His workshop, even subordinating to his will all the phenomena of creation. If this Maker were then to decree that the whole existence of man should come to an end with his death, He would render fruitless and meaningless the very foundation for the existence of the world and the presence in it of so noble a creature as man.

However, based on the principle of growth towards perfection, the attainment of everlasting life represents the last stage of perfection. Otherwise, what grow would it be that after traversing a whole series of motions and changes the final destiny of all beings should be annihilation? For what is implied by the principle is progress and advancement, not change and development leading to nothing. Even a cyclical concept of motion and change would be meaningless, because it too would lack a final outcome and goal.

Apart from all this, human knowledge and science exclude the possibility of absolute annihilation for any phenomenon whatsoever; given the imperishability of matter and energy, the material particles that make up this world cannot be destroyed within the context of the present order of things.

All things will attain the perfection they seek when another order, based in immortality and eternity, comes to prevail over the scattered elements of this world, irrespective of whether the universal movement towards perfection takes place in the outer form of things or in their essence and content.

This comprehensive process of change, this permanent motion, becomes rationally acceptable and capable of being correctly understood only when it has a direction and an aim toward which it advances.

With its regular and precisely calculated motion, the entirety of the universe is moving forward to its final maturity – i.e., resurrection – just like a child advancing to the higher stage of development that maturity represents. In short, the universal and innate progress of all things from defectiveness to a series of relative perfections has as its aim absolute perfection, just as the Qur'ān declares: "*To Him you will return*" (10:4).

Thus not only does the wheel of material progress never stop, and the entirety of the universe never cease advancing. At the same time, man's inner and spiritual progress and his lofty ideals cannot be completed under the conditions of his present existence. It is in fact the ending of the present order of things that brings about the beginning of his eternal life and the conditions that are required for him to attain lofty degree and sublime station. Freed from all kinds of material impurity, he discovers for himself a realm overflowing with both material and spiritual pleasure; it is there that his faith and deeds come to bear fruit, and everyone is requited for his convictions and acts.

Thus the Qur'ān says: "*We did not create the heavens and the earth and all they contain in vain and for no purpose"* (28:27).

"*Those who in all states — standing, sitting, or lying — remember God and reflect constantly on the creation of the heavens and the earth, and say, 'O Creator, you did not create this magnificent universe in vain; You are pure and exalted; preserve us from hellfire through Your grace'"* (3:191).

"*We did not create as a game the heavens and the earth and all they contain; We created them in justice and in accordance with wisdom, but most men know not"* (44:38-39).

The one who is convinced of the far-reaching wisdom of God knows that in this vast arena where all things are uniquely submitted to His preeternal power nothing is left to its own devices or lacks fixed, defined content. He knows that the order of the world in nurtured by perfect wisdom and justice and that all the phenomena it contains are constantly changing and advancing in accordance with an orderly, harmonious, and ineluctable pattern.

Were rebellion and the violation of law to be the principle governing the universe, were the foundation of all existent things to be error, there would be no sign of harmony or orderliness in the world, and in fact we would be obliged to condemn the whole world to non-existence.

The believer in God's wisdom knows that he possesses himself the means of cultivating the inner world that will last unto eternity; he can either build and cultivate his future life, or set it ablaze and turn it into a ruin.

So if man has such a concept of the universe, he will never imagine that all dimensions of human existence are annihilated once this life comes to an end. He understands that the present order of things continues in a profound sense, in a form that is both appropriate and glorious, and that it is within that transformed order of things that his thirst for exalted values and ideals may be finally quenched.

The infinite essence of God is perfect in every respect; lack and need cannot assail His sacred being. It is, on the contrary, created things that stand in need of Him. God bestows the blessings of life, together with all powers and faculties, on man, and it is but natural that the final outcome of His creation should revert to Him. Thus the Qur'ān says: "*O mankind, you stand in need of God; it is only His unique essence that is absolutely free of all need*" (35:15).

* * * * *

God's wisdom thus necessitates that on a certain day men should be called to account for their deeds. The Qur'ān promises that such a day will come: "*Of a certainty, God will gather all His creatures on the day of resurrection, all His deeds are inspired by knowledge and wisdom*" (15:25).

The ultimate perfection of which man is truly worthy is not attainable in the sphere of this world. His growth towards perfection continues until in the afterlife he reaches his ultimate aim and desire, which is the attainment of union with the sublime origin of all being.

Men will come to meet their Creator in a way determined by their deeds, characteristics, and their conduct in this world. This is true both of the pure and the fortunate and of the wretched whose hearts are blackened with sin. For all creatures must inevitable submit to the irresistible will of God and the unfailing norms He has established; willingly or not, they return to Him. However, the way in which they meet God is determined by their conduct while in this world and the attributes they have acquired. Once the deeds of men reach their conclusion, the results of their acts are revealed and become apparent. The quality of men's meeting with God depends, then, on the mode of behavior that has distinguished and characterised them in this world.

Thus the Qur'ān proclaims: "*O man! To the degree that you strive to obey God you will in the end meet your Creator*" (84:6).

"*Your ending will be with God Almighty*" (53:42).

"*He is God Whose might and power are supreme over His servants. He sends angels as guards to watch over you, so that when the time for the death of one among you arrives Our messengers drive him forth. They show no lassitude in taking your soul. Then you will return to the Lord of the Universe Who is in reality the master of His servants. Be aware that judgement over mankind belongs to God, and He is swifter than anyone in calling to account*" (6:61-62).

As for those black-hearted ones who are destined for hellfire, they too come face to face with the Most Sacred Essence of God. However, God does not look upon them with favor and mercy, and they are deprived of His favor.

The Qur'ān says: "*There shall be no share for them on the day of resurrection: God will not speak to them or look in their direction*" (3:77).

"*The faces of one group of men will be luminous and smiling on the day when they meet God, while the faces of another group will be as if covered with dust: mired in shame, these will be the unbelievers, evil in conduct*" (80:38-42).

Man possesses lofty religious and moral instincts that draw him to God. Under the influence of these instincts he will come to believe in God desire to cross the boundaries which imprison him throughout his material life. Accordingly, he will eagerly and in a spirit of high aspiration renounce the outer, material life of this world for the sake of great goals and valuable ideals.

Such a transformation in his outlook is made possible by the fact that an eternal ideal wells up from his being and that he possesses lofty instincts which are related to eternity. Those instincts draw him in the direction of eternity so that ultimately he enters his true realm. All of this means that there is innate within man the capacity for life everlasting.

The deeds and conduct of man are like a seed from which eternal life grows, a seed that can flourish and develop only in a life of eternal bliss. The seeds that evildoers plant in this world also earn them a from of eternal life, one in which they reap the fruits of their evil.

'Alī b. Abī Ṭālib, the Commander of the Faithful, peace be upon him, remarked in this connection: "The world is a place of passage and the hereafter a place of abode."[6]

It is in truth the hereafter that gives meaning to the life of this world.

Lesson Four
Resurrection, a
Manifestation of Divine Justice

The question of divine justice – a question which has numerous dimensions – must be raised at this point.

We observe that in this world the good and evil deeds of men are not subject to any final accounting. Criminals and oppressive rulers, who with their claim to absolute sovereignty encroach on men's lives and their freedom, may enjoy opulence and luxury until the end of their lives. They shun no action that their polluted minds inspire in them, but they are not caught in the firm grasp of justice and law, and they do not suffer the natural consequences of their deeds. There is no power or authority to prevent their oppression, to stop their encroachment on the rights of others, or to restrict the scope of their power to their own private affairs.

In the end both the oppressor and the oppressed, the one polluted with sin, and the wise one who strives to gain mastery over his passionate instincts and acquire virtue, who attains abundant spirituality through the admixture of piety to his conduct – all will close their eyes on the world. It is true that religion forbids all forms of submission to unbelieving rulers and the acceptance of the tyrannical edicts put forth by oppressive governments, and that it regards resistance to all kinds of aggression as a neccessary dictate of religion and life. Nonetheless, confrontation with oppressors does not always yield a positive result, and in the course of the struggle people may be trampled by the power of the oppressors and lose their lives. Were the file to be closed in this world on the deeds of the good and the evil so that they were buried for ever in the cemetery of nothingness, what would become of the infinite justice, wisdom, and mercy that God cherishes for His servants – God, the traces of whose justice and wisdom are manifest throughout His creation?

If we accept that God has created an environment in which numerous evildoers and oppressors are able to continue on their chosen path until the last moment of their lives, without recognizing any limit on their behavior, to stoop to any vile act in order to gain power and gratify their desires – if we accept that this is possible without their being called to account, and that the oppressed continue to writhe beneath the lash of injustice and deprivation until their last gasp – can all of this be called anything but oppression and injustice?

Now we know that nobody who has the slightest notion of love and justice would consent to such a state of affairs; how then could the most Sacred Essence of God, from Whose being infinite pity, love, and justice flow forth, accept such injustice and place on it His seal of approval? How would the creative mind of man, the most sublime aspect of his being that guides him to knowledge of himself and the universe judge this matter?

It is true that God has not directly permitted the commission of a cruelty against a given person. However, the fact that a certain collectivity grants some criminal oppressor the freedom and power to act as he wills and in the end exempts him from all punishment is in itself a clear form of injustice. The link between God's justice and the need for a precise accounting of men's deeds thus makes irrefutably clear the necessity for resurrection.

In addition, certain crimes and evils are so extensive in their effects that they cannot be adequately punished in this world, with its limited timespan. Crimes are sometimes so grave that the punishment inflicted by men is not equal to the task of imposing on the criminal the punishment he deserves. The criminal plunderer for whom the world is nothing but a carcass on which to feed kills and consumes at will; his hands are stained with the blood of hundreds or thousands of people whom he drags into the slaughterhouse. He is so sunk in the mire of vice and injustice that he is incapable of learning lessons from the past or thinking of a better and more enlightened future. If despite all his crimes his soul were to be taken in just the same way as that of one of his victims, the punishment involved would be unjust and grossly unequal, for he would then have been punished simply for one of his victims and all his other crimes would remain unpunished.

Many crimes are, then, beyond the scope of worldly retribution. If we wish to analyse matters more logically, we must look further, beyond this world. There is also the consideration that no authority in this world has the power to restore to men all the rights which have been violated.

Similarly, the world does not have the capacity to reward virtue in a fitting and complete manner. When we attempt to assess the value of the unrelenting efforts that the pure and the virtuous expend in this world, which is full of trouble and pain, we realise that the rewards available here are very slight.

What reward commensurate with the value of his efforts can be given in this world to one who has benefited millions of people with his treasury of knowledge and learning or sincere and devoted service?

How and where in this world will one be rewarded who devotes all his life to the worship of God and the support of His servants, whose services extend in manifold ways to whole societies, and who ultimately gives up his life for the sake of divine goals?

No life remains for him in this world to enable him to reap the fruits of his devotion and self-sacrifice. The temporal limitation imposed on life in this world does not even permit the pious to receive their reward.

The Qur'ān says. "*Shall We make those who believe in God and do good deeds like those who work corruption on earth? Shall We require pious and Godfearing men like the sinful and the doers of evil?*

Do those who have committed foul and sinful deeds imagine that We will grant them a rank like that of those who believe in God and do good works, so that they will be alike in death and in life? Theirs is a false and ignorant notion. God has created the heavens and the earth in justice, and ultimately every soul shall receive the requital for its deeds, without any injustice" (45:21-22).

From the day that he first steps into this abode of dust until the moment the earth draws him into its embrace, man has to struggle with hardships, difficulties, problems and misfortunes.

The Commander of the Faithful, 'Alī, peace be upon him, depicts this transient, pain-filled world as follows:

"The world is a dwelling the inhabitants of which are overcome by sorrow and pain. It is a world well-known for its deceit and trickery and lacking in all stability. Those who enter this dwelling will never enjoy safety or tranquillity. Its circumstances are constantly changing, and its pleasures are reprehensible and blameworthy. Repose and tranquillity are nowhere to be found in it. Every instant it fires the arrow of disaster at man, before finally despatching him to the jaws of death and destruction."

Can it be believed that such a world, replete with pain, misfortune and hardship, should be the final aim and goal of creation? That a God all of Whose actions are based on excellence and order and the signs of Whose justice and wisdom are manifest throughout creation, should have created man only for the sake of such a world?

Comprehensive and Universal Order

It must be remarked at this point that the order we see in the world is a divine order, one that includes all things in its scope. All created objects in the universe, whether large or small, ranging from the minute particles of the atom to the countless planets that are scatterred throughout space, are created and take form from the justice that rules the whole scheme of creation. This vast system of being does not escape the direct influence of the rule of justice for a single instant;

this is a reality that can be deduced from all the phenomena in the world of creation.

Should the component parts of this system deviate even so slightly from their prescribed orbit, the necessary principles on which the order, of the universe is based would collapse, resulting in its destruction.

Despite all his remarkable talents, man forms a part of this universal order; he cannot be regarded as exempt from its comprehensive and universal rules. The only factor that sets him apart is his possession of freedom which enables him to be creative and inventive; it opens up before him a path for attaining his goals and purposes. It is indeed a source of pride for him that alone among all the creatures of the phenomenal world he is able — thanks to this unique quality and the potentialities it yields — to tame his destructive impulses and reconcile them with his constructive activities. By creating man free, God has demonstrated both the underlying order of the universe and the changes that are brought about in that order by the disobedience of man.

Were man to be directed ineluctably toward the acquisition of spiritual riches and the path leading to happiness, were a deterministic power to conduct him toward lofty values, there would be no pride in this for man. We must therefore accept that by receiving the gift of freedom and will from God, man must one day stand in the court of God's justice to be judged there according to the universal principle of all creation — justice. It cannot be believed that man should be exempt from the justice of the Creator that prevails throughout the universe, thus becoming an element of disharmony.

If we take into consideration on the hand the functioning of the principle of justice throughout the entire scheme of being and on the other hand the fact that many rewards and punishments cannot be dispensed in this world, it becomes obvious that the nature of men's deeds and accomplishments must by subjected to examination in another world and at an appropriate time. The proof lies in the deduction that can be made from man's essential nature (as a being possessing freedom), for all the dimensions of his being, all his ideals and fundamental needs, will come to fruition in the hereafter.

Thus we can understand well that God Who has no need for the creation of man will never destroy or obliterate our being before it attains perfection. This is unthinkable, and no intelligent person would consent to such an erroneous notion.

The Requital of Deeds

It is obvious that the deeds of all sinners cannot be fully requited in this world. Nonetheless, some punishments do occur in this world, as can be seen from those pages of history which record the disastrous fate of certain wrongdoers. Indeed we ourselves witness time and again the bitter and painful fates they undergo; after suffering torment and humiliation, they go to their deaths in utter disgrace, although no one had been able to predict such an inauspicious end for those powerful tyrants.

The existence of such a remarkable linkage between corrupt action and ultimate disgrace cannot be ascribed to simple coincidence; it must on the contrary be regarded as an instance of requital taking place in this world.

The Qur'ān says: "*God will cause them to taste humiliation in this world, and the torment of the hereafter will be much greater, if they but knew*" (39:26).

Such chastisements sometimes function as alarm bells, as warnings to the sinners, encouraging them to come to their senses, to change direction and reform themselves before it is too late. These warnings remind them that good and evil are the two pans of the balance in which our deeds will be weighed, and that no abomination or moral corruption will go unpunished, in just the same way that no good deed will remain unrewarded.

A Western philosopher writes:

"The world resembles a multiplication table; however much you manipulate it, it retains its structure and shape and always yields the same answer. Whatever method we may choose to solve a mathematical problem, the figures that result will be the same. Nature silently but ineluctably reveals all secrets: it punishes every crime, rewards every virtue, and compensates for every act of oppression.

"What we call retribution is a universal need; it causes the whole to appear from within its constituent part. If we see smoke, we are certain that it has arisen from fire, and if we see a hand or a foot we have no doubt that it is attached to a body.

"Every act carries its own requital. To put it differently, in accordance with the law of which we have spoken, every act completes itself in two ways: first by way of action and reaction within the thing itself, in its objective nature, and then with respect to its outer qualities. What we mean by outer qualities is none other than what is commonly called retribution and punishment. The retribution that takes place in the thing itself can be seen with the eye; the retribution that takes place in the external quality of a thing is visible only to the intelligence. This second form of retribution is inseparable from the thing itself, and may not become apparent for some time.

"The consequences peculiar to a given sin may appear years after the sin was committed, but they will definitely occur because they are inherently attached to it, like the branch of tree to its trunk. Alternatively we may say that both crime and punishment are the branches of a single trunk. Retribution is the fruit that suddenly emerges from the blossom of the pleasure that the sin yields."[8]

* * * * *

The appearance of the consequences of evil acts is a clear sign that God Almighty does not accept corruption and wrongdoing, and that all sinners will receive their due punishment in the next world.

In addition, the positive educational effect of requital should not be underestimated, both on the individual and on society. The whiplash of punishment should from this point of view be regarded as a form of mercy and divine favor, leading to men's awakening and their aspiring to purity. It is a form of compensation the payment of which earns men abundant benefit.

In order for His justice to reach the fullest extent possible, God has freed man of the shadow of determinism and granted him the divine trust which even the mountains had been unwilling to bear. Ascent to the lofty station of true humanity is possible only through effort and striving, by passing through the furnace of trial. The Qur'ān says: "*Every man is a pledge for his own deeds*" (74: 38).

What is meant by this is that whatever appears in this world in the form of a sin or misdeed takes on in the hereafter the shape of the implementation of justice and the punishment of the transgressor. It is belief in the pre-eternal source of all existence and His all-embracing justice that impels man to act correctly and with justice himself.

Imām al-Sajjād, upon whom be peace, made this supplication to God:

"O God, I know that there is no cruelty or oppression in any of Your decrees or commands, and that You do not hasten to punish anyone, for only he hastens to perform an act who fears he may miss the opportunity, and only he who is weak and impotent feels the need to commit oppression and cruelty. You, O Creator, are pure and exalted above both these defects."[9]

A theologian says:

"It is better for all mankind that they spend their lives in the service of the One God, for the spirit that serves God is the legitimate commander of the body, and the mind that serves God brings under control the passions and unruly emotions of man. I ask therefore what justice can possibly exist in the person who does not serve God. It can plainly be seen that such an individual does not rule over his bodily form by means of his spirit, nor over his emotions by means of his intellect."[10]

For those who do serve God the ideal life is that which comes after death. As the Qur'ān says: "*The hereafter is the abode of true life, and the life of this world is but play and amusement*" (29:64).

Those devoted to God not only do not fear death, but even wait longingly for the moment that the angel of death shall whisper melodiously in their ear: "*O sacred spirit, return to your Creator, satisfied and well-pleased*" (89:27-28).

These verses of the Qur'ān are also relevant:

"*On that day your journeying shall bring you to the presence of your Lord*" (75:12).

"*Your return will be to your Lord*" (96:8).

"*There is none in the heavens and the earth but will come before God as His servant. He is aware of the number of all His creation, and they shall all individually be present before Him on the day of resurrection*" (19:93-95).

In the other realm happiness will be the essential goal of all beings, and pleasures will be available for them that we cannot even imagine.

In short, this life full of confusion and oppression is only a small part of the totality of life. One group will earn as the final result of its deeds permanent abode in the propinquity of God's mercy, while another group will find itself condemned to be the neighbors of Iblīs in eternal torment. Are these two destinies in any way equal – the misery of hellfire and the blessing of paradise? It is up to man to choose freely between them.

Lesson Five
Man's Essential Nature
as Evidence for Resurrection

If we look at religion from the viewpoint of the history of human society, we will see that at every stage of human thought, in the mists of prehistory as well as throughout the broad expanse of recorded history of this changing world, man has always firmly believed in a life after death.

When we follow archeologists in their excavations, we find material traces of primitive men who all believed in a life after the life of this world. The tools and implements they buried with their dead bear witness to the distinctive conceptions they held of the life that exists behind the gate of death. They knew that death is not the end of all life, but because of their erroneous concepts they imagined that man would need the tools of life in the next world just as he does in this, and that he would be able to use the implements buried with him.

In whatever land and age he has lived, man has always had a hidden perception, a kind of inspiration, that permits him to hope for a tomorrow after today. Some monodimensional sociologists fail to grasp this truth, with their purely rationalistic interpretations, and they discuss the matter purely in the light of social and economic factors. Concentrating on the fantastic and superstitious aspects of certain religions, they overlook the positive dimensions of belief in the hereafter.

These profound and well-rooted beliefs cannot be taken simply as the result of autopersuasion or habit, for habit and custom cannot resist for ever time and the changes that it brings in human society.

Although the peoples of the world differ in their national and social customs because of ethnic and natural variation, so that each people has its own special customs and habits of thought, all men hold in common a certain set of instincts and attributes.

Whatever country or continent they inhabit, all men — even semi-barbaric, backward, and prehistoric peoples — respect and value precious concepts such as justice, equity and trustworthiness, just as they shun and abhor treachery, cruelty and anarchic behavior.

So although destructive changes and revolutions may overturn and obliterate many of the habits and customs that have ruled for centuries over a given society, so that not even a trace is left of them today, the attachment and respect that men of the past nurtured for virtues such as justice, generosity, and trustworthiness remains exactly the same today in every human society. It can even be said that the flame of men's love for these concepts burns more brightly today and that their attachment to them is more profound than ever before.

Purely social conventions must be learned by children when their intellect and powers of discernment begin to blossom; by contrast, instinctual and natural urges emerge from the inner being of the child without any need for a teacher or master.

Being inherent to man and firmly rooted in his nature, belief in eternal truths and the awareness of creation and resurrection have proven immune to all the changes that human societies have undergone in history; they are permanent and stable.

Those who bury their heads in the sand of fantasy are merely trying to cover up one of the most profound perceptions of man with their baseless and often incomprehensible imaginings.

* * * * *

Some form of belief in the hereafter existed among the Romans, the Egyptians, the Greeks, the Babylonians the Chaldaeans, and the other peoples of the ancient world, although the belief was often superficial, tainted with superstition, and far removed from the logic of a true faith in God's unity. The same is true of the beliefs of certain primitive peoples. For example, it was customary among some tribes on the Congo that when one of their kings died, twelve virgins would present themselves at his grave and then begin fighting and arguing for the privilege of being joined with the deceased, often with fatal results! The people of the Fiji Islands believed that the dead engage in all the same activities as the living -- fighting battles, procreating children, tilling the land, and so on.

A scholar writes:

"One of the customs of the people of Fiji is that they bury their mothers and fathers when they reach the age of forty. The reason for selecting this age as the age of burial is that it is the approximate middle of life, the most desirable of ages, so that when the deceased is resurrected, he will find himself in possession of the physical strength he had when he was forty years old."[11]

Samuel King, the well-known sociologist, says:

"Religion not only exists today throughout the world; careful research also shows that the most primitive tribes also possessed a form of religion. Neanderthal man — the ancestor of present-day humanity — clearly had some form of religion because we know that he used to bury his dead in a certain way, placing their tools and implements beside them and thus demonstrating belief in a future world."[12]

The people of Mexico used to bury the court jester together with the king, so that he might amuse the dead sovereign in the grave and dispel his sorrow with his antics and jokes!

The Greeks of three thousand years ago believed that man does not disappear when he dies; he continues living like the people of this world with exactly the same needs. They therefore placed food next to their graves.[13]

Although certain beliefs concerning the nature of the afterlife may then be tainted with superstition or form a mixture of truth and falsehood, the persistence of the belief itself throughout time confirms that it has an inner core which is inherent to man's nature. It is nurtured by inspiration and inward perception and is embedded in the structure of man's being.

It is also beyond doubt that the knowledge of man is based on certain self-evident first premises; if these are subjected to doubt, the authority to which all of man's knowledge goes back will be shaken, and no reliance can be placed on any knowledge at all. The witness borne by man's innermost, primordial nature constitutes, in fact, the highest form of evidence, and no logic can contest it.

Without having any need for deduction and proof, we can understand, aided by our primordial disposition, that the order of being is based on justice and accountability. Whatever arises from our essence is part of our being and part of the order of creation, an order that admits of no error. It is the inward nature of man that makes it possible for him to arrive at the truth.

When our instinctive awareness and our nature inspire in us the knowledge that answerability, accounting, and law exist in the universe, when our primordial disposition issues a judgement to this effect, we have in fact acquired a decisive proof that is superior to empirically attained certainty, for we perceive the certainty and inevitability of resurrection with full clarity once we understand it by means of our inner nature.

We feel clearly that unaccountability and meaninglessness have no foundation in the objective world. Firm laws regulate all existing things, from the minute particles of the atom to the vast heavenly bodies. The birth and death of planets and stars, the transformation of the mass of the sun into luminous energy, all take place by way of an equation. The different forms of organic matter each have their own lines of attraction, and nothing goes to waste, even the energy of one part of an atom. In short, the entire order of creation follows an unvarying regularity; it is like a table of firm and unbending laws.

Why then does the behavior of men deviate from the normative orbit of all beings? Why is it not based on justice and regularity, and why do injustice, disorder, and lack of restraint, rage unchecked in the human realm?

The answer is obvious: that we are differentiated from all other creatures by being endowed with the blessing of consciousness and free will.

The scope of our acts is extremely wide. If God had wished, He could have compelled us to obey natural law, but His far-reaching wisdom caused Him to make us His viceregents on earth and to grant us freedom. To act injustly or irresponsibly is, therefore, to misuse this freedom we have been given, to pervert it in the most irrational way.

Since this world is a place of trial and testing, enabling us to pass on to the stages of existence that yet await us, it cannot be thought that this passing life, full of cruelty oppression, and the violation of rights, represents the entirety of life. In reality, it is a single chapter in a long story that continues until infinity.

Our innate feelings inform us that the oppressor who escapes worldly justice, the aggressor who tramples on the rights of men and is not caught in the trap of the law, the criminal who is able to ensure that the provisions of justice are not implemented in his case — all such people will ultimately be prosecuted by the principle of justice that underlies the entire universe.

The necessity and inevitability of justice in the order of creation brings man to believe that one day a precise accounting will take place in utter justice.

Were true justice to be nothing but an imaginary ideal and our hearts' belief in it to lack all reality, why should we instinctively desire justice for ourselves and for others? Why should we be angered by the sight of rights being violated and even be ready to sacrifice our own beings for the sake of justice? Why should the love of justice be so deeply rooted in our hearts and why should we expect something that does not even exist? Is not our thirsting for justice in itself a proof that justice does in fact exist, just as our thirsting for water is an indication that water exists?

The Desire for Immortality

The desire for eternal life is also something fundamental to man, embedded in his essential nature. The concept of immortality is not an accidental or acquired desire; on the contrary, this profound longing proves in itself that man has the capacity and readiness for eternal life. Every natural inclination is satisfied in the appropriate way within the order of creation; to desire permanent life in this impermanent world is by contrast a desire that is unnatural and cannot therefore be satisfied.

Just as it is not possible for man totally to extinguish the flame of his inner nature and to forget utterly his innate inclination to the source of being, so that his mind instinctively turns towards that Unique Essence whenever he is assailed by the trials and hardships of life, so too those who deny the hereafter unconsciously acquire a desire for eternal life whenever they are faced with an impasse in their lives.

As soon as man gains some respite from the turmoil of material life and has the opportunity to reflect and turn inwards, he begins to think of life after death and to feel keenly the emptiness of this impermanent, transitory world.

Once animals satisfy all their material needs, they are at rest. By contrast, once man is satiated with material pleasures and bodily enjoyments, he begins to feel unease in himself. A mysterious pain troubles his soul. Many people who find themselves in this position have recourse to distractions and entertainment in order to flee from their inner disquiet and to obtain at least temporary relief from the grief that is caused by thoughts of the future.

Many, too, are those who find in suicide their only escape from this excruciating torment.

Great men and thinkers have always decried the life of this world, with its mixture of pleasure and pain, of joy and sadness. We cannot find a single person among the prophets, the saints, and the major figures of religion, who regarded the world as a suitable or ideal place for man to reside.

There are many people who verbally deny belief in resurrection and the day of judgement, but at the same they strive to leave a good name behind when they die. Why should someone who regards death as the end of all things be concerned for his good repute or for acts of charity that outlive him?

There is no point in expending such effort for something that has no reality; once life has come to an end, how can a scientific achievement, an act of charity, a work of art, benefit one who denies all form of life after death?

Such a person is acting, in reality, according to the desire of his innermost being; he is demonstrating that in fact he does believe in his own immortality.

* * * * *

The scope of man's desires and aspirations is unbounded so that if one day he comes to master the whole world, his unquiet spirit will still find no rest; he will then begin thinking of conquering the planets. If hypothetically he were to attain that goal also, some mysterious inward feeling would still rob him of peace and tranquillity.

Man also recognizes no boundary or limit in the acquisition of knowledge. In fact, with every step that he takes in increasing his knowledge, his desire to discover still more also increases. The whole universe cannot fully accommodate man's aspirations to explore, despite its seemingly boundless expanse, for the infinite spirit of man cannot be contained by the heavens and the earth. Man accepts no limit for his desires short of the fulfilment of his desire for immortality, enabling him to gain his true ultimate goal.

Thus a wise poet says, identifying himself with Mawlānā
Jalāl ad-Dīn Rūmī:

My spirit is ascending to the throne of the Beloved;
  "Rumi" and "Balkhi" are simply two skins in my view.
Although my body travelled from Khorasan to Rum,
  My spirit cannot be contained by any land.
Do not imagine that I am some earthworm;
  I am of the heavens, not of the earth.

In order for this natural impulse in man to be satisfied, the
necessary means must exist; would it be possible, by way of
analogy, for water not to exist in the external world to satisfy
the instinct of thirst?

Certain conditions must exist for the satisfaction of this
profound feeling in man, this ideal and aspiration for eternal
life. Were the means and conditions needed to satisfy the
inward inclinations and aspirations that aré rooted in everyone
not to exist, man would fall prey to bewilderment and
confusion. All his hopes and aspirations would be based on
illusion and vanity. We see, however, that in the whole orderly
system of the universe not even a single phenomenon can be
glimpsed that is irregular or misplaced.

We can assert, therefore, that no inclination or desire that
is rooted in man's essential nature is vain and purposeless, and
that this being the case the essence of man's being is not
annihilated when he steps through the gateway of death. On
the contrary, it is in the hereafter that his desire for eternal life
is fulfilled.

Dr. Norman Vincent, a European (?) scholar, writes:

"I have never had the slightest doubt or hesitation
concerning everlasting life; I believe in it and consider it
irrefutable.

"Man's innate sentiment of everlasting life is one of the
most important and positive proofs that guide us to an
appreciation of this truth. When God Almighty wishes to guide
man to a certain truth, He first sows the seed of it in his
innermost consciousness. Man's thirst for eternity is so
universal that it is inadmissible that it should remain

unfulfilled.

"It is not through mathematical proofs that man comes to accept metaphysical truths; it is faith and inspiration that convince him of them. In fact, inspiration plays an important role even in the realm of scientific truths."[14]

A group of scholars reached the following conclusion after investigating men's beliefs in the hereafter:

"The truth of the matter is that faith and inward belief in life after death constitute the best and strongest proof for the reality of the hereafter.

"Whenever God wishes to convince the spirit of man of a certain matter, He inserts the causes and factors of the belief among man's own instincts. It is because of this wise act of the Creator that everyone perceives eternal existence and life everlasting in the depths of his own soul. Since such permanent life is not feasible under the present conditions of man's existence, a different set of conditions is needed for this aspiration to be realized. This universal consciousness of immortality is so profound and well rooted that its reality and remarkable effects on human life cannot be overlooked. From the most ancient times down to the present, it has caused belief in resurrection to remain alive and vigorous in the minds of men."[15]

* * * * *

An emphatic belief in life everlasting is to be found on every page of the history of the major religions; it forms an inseparable part of every divinely inspired religion. This matter has occupied so important a place in the mission of the prophets that no messenger has ever arisen without preparing his followers for a future in which they will be rewarded or punished for their deeds.

In order to complete His favor and grace, God the Creator and Inspirer of all beings, Who looks upon His servants with infinite mercy and kindness, has not only placed within man a form of inward guidance and enlightenment; He has also sent prophets, equipped with books and proofs, whose duty it is to guide men to perceiving the reality of resurrection. This is necessary because passionate desires and idiosyncracies as well as material inclinations dull the lustre of man's primordial nature, so that the guide within man's own being cannot ensure alone man's ascent to the lofty rank of true humanity and his deliverance from the barriers that stand in his way.

The Qur'ān says:

"Never imagine that God will violate the promises made by His messengers. God is certainly empowered over all things and will take vengeance on the oppressors. On the day when the earth and the heavens are transformed, so that all creatures will stand before the One God, Powerful and Invincible, you will see the evildoers and the rebellious chained by God's wrath, wearing shirts of molten brass, and their faces will be hidden by fire.

"This torment is so that God may punish men for their misdeeds, for God will make His reckoning in a single instant. This is a declaration to all mankind, so that they should take heed and be aware, recognizing their Lord as their only object of worship" (14:47-52).

Lesson Six
Scientific Indications of Resurrection

One of the valuable benefits that have been derived from the ceaseless progress of experimental science is that it has proven the possibility of the man's restoration to life. The advancement of human knowledge has, in fact, opened up a very interesting area of exploration in this respect, placing the matter in a new light and making it possible to examine it with precision for the very first time. This achievement contributes significantly to an improved understanding of the topic, and it appears, moreover, that scientific investigations of the matter are advancing toward still more highly developed theories. The broader the scope of science becomes, the fewer ambiguities and obscurities will remain in this area.

When early materialist scholars discussed the question of resurrection, they regarded a return to life as impossible, and were therefore unable to treat resurrection as a topic worthy of scientific discussion.

The first change that occurred as a result of continuing scientific investigations of the matter was brought about by Lavoisier, the celebrated French scholar and founder of modern chemistry. He refuted previous theories and brought their dominance to an end, because in the course of the researches to which he devoted the major part of his life he reached the conclusion that the total quantity and mass of matter in the world are stable, subject to neither decrease nor increase.

The discovery of radioactivity and the transformation of matter into energy – the second important advance that was achieved in this area – caused Lavoisier's law to be modified, but it has retained its validity as far as the permanence of matter and energy is concerned.

Despite the chemical action and reaction which take place in the matter of which the world is composed, causing it to change its form and shape, no element of matter is ever buried in the cemetery of annihilation. What we see and perceive is a collection of various beings possessing mutable qualities. Thus the theory of the indestructability of being came to replace the previous law and to explain fully all the changes and transformations that take place in matter.

A drop of water that falls on the ground and is absorbed; the smoke of a cigarette that rises in the air; the various fuels that are consumed by industrial machinery; the flame that arises from burning dry wood; the candle that burns, scattering its particles in the air – none of this is utterly lost and destroyed. If we had the means of reassembling their component parts we would obtain the same original materials, without the slightest decrease. It is only our superficial way of viewing things, our limited and inadequate way of thinking, that makes us imagine all these things disappear.

* * * * *

Man's body is formed of clay, and after passing beneath the wheels of change and transformation it changes back into clay; i.e., it returns to its original form. This is because the body carries within it receptivity to change within it, but its existential core never tends to non-being as a result of these changes. It loses only the particular nature of its composition, like all other bodies, without ever sacrificing anything of its essence.

Similarly, the dead and lifeless form of man is transformed into clay, through the working of internal and external factors; it turns this way and that, each time assuming a new form. For example, in the course of time, a plant may grow from the soil where a person is buried and be eaten by an animal, contributing to its growth. Thus variety has been introduced into the matter of which man's body is composed, but the substance and content of his body remain firm and indestructible throughout all the changes that may occur.

The different forms taken on by our energy — good and bad deeds — are likewise imbued with stability and permanence; they are preserved in the archives of the universe as the determining factor in our ultimate fate, whether it be good or evil, eternal happiness or permanent torment. We are obliged to submit to the consequences of our deeds.

The efforts of researchers to capture the sound waves emitted by men of the past have enjoyed some success; to a limited degree and with the aid of special equipment they have been able to recapture the sound waves emitted by the makers of tools, imprinted on the surface of those tools by the radiation of their hands.

These scientific accomplishments are in themselves an indication of the reality of resurrection; they provide a method which joined together with reflection may permit us to understand resurrection and prove it scientifically.

Quite apart from all the foregoing, we may ask why God should not be able to recreate the form of man which came into being out of scattered particles of clay and was then again turned into earth.

The Qur'ān makes repeated reference to this matter, saying for example: "*We created you from earth and return you to earth, and then bring you forth from it once more*" (20:55).

In this verse, our attention is drawn to the creative power of the Maker. Through the presentation of the past and future of man in this world and the hereafter in a single panorama, solace and assurance are given to man's unquiet and sceptical soul. The thought of man being swallowed up in death is shown to be irrational, and to speak of the changes and transformations that man undergoes as aimless is demonstrated to be absurd.

Life in the narrow sphere of this world is too petty to

represent the ultimate aim of creation. If we take into consideration the total picture of creation, we will see that this petty realm taken in isolation is unworthy of the lofty origins from which it sprang.

Addressing those incredulous people who imagine that the body of man dissolves and disappears as a result of chemical actions and reactions within the soil and that it cannot be restored to life, the Qur'ān says: "*The unbelievers say: 'Is this not a strange thing that we should be brought back after dying and turning to dust? Such a return is impossible.' But We are fully aware of what the earth takes from them, and it is We Who possess the Preserved Tablet*" (50:2-4).

This verse refers, then, to a group of unbelievers who deny the resurrection of the dead. It reminds them that God knows full well where the elements are that once made up their bodies before being dispersed and returned to the storehouse of nature. He will reassemble those elements on the plain of resurrection, thus reconstructing the body in a way the unbelievers thought impossible. This reconstruction will follow entirely the structure and contents of the body as it previously existed and be based entirely upon it.

The Persuasive Logic of the Qur'ān

When the Prophet of Islam, peace and blessings be upon him and his family, expounded the topic of resurrection to the pagan Arabs, a Bedouin by the name of Ubayy b. Khalaf picked up a decayed bone and set out for Medina to visit the Prophet. In the hope of refuting the arguments of the Prophet and the logic of the Qur'ān on which they were based, he raised up the bone, as if it were a valuable and convincing piece of evidence, and crumbled it to dust, scattering the pieces in the air. Then, he addressed to the Prophet these crude, unadorned words, inspired by his rebelliousness and ignorance:

"Who will restore to life the scattered particles of this rotten bone?"

He believed that he would thus be able to refute the arguments of the Prophet and to destroy the belief of others in resurrection of the dead. His ignorant mode of thought prevented him from having any correct notion of the creation of being so that he imagined that the scattered particles of a decayed bone could not possibly be brought back to life. He obstinately maintained that the reassembling of the countless particles of the body was unacceptable to man's reason.

The Qur'ān replied with this convincing argument based on persuasive logic: "*(O Messenger,) say: 'God Who first brought them to life will restore them to life. He has knowledge of all His creation.'* . . . *Is the Creator Who brought into being the heavens and the earth incapable of creating the like thereof? Certainly He is the Creator and All-Knowing*" (36:79, 81).

*   *   *   *   *

The Qur'ān invites man to contemplate, the whole vast structure of creation, together with the innumerable phenomena and minutiae it contains, using his wisdom and intelligence which are his means for recognizing the principles underlying the universe. Such reflection will enable him to realize that the restoration of life to man through resurrection is not more difficult than the initial creation out of a mass of different materials that were compounded together.

It is thought and reflection that lead to correct comprehension; they form the method by which man must acquire a true understanding of the world in which he lives and they confirm, in a logical and profound fashion, the concepts he holds.

The Qur'ān stresses the importance of resurrection as follows: "*Were We weakened by bringing forth creation the first time that We should now be incapable of restoring it to life through resurrection?*" (50:15).

The Qur'ān wishes man to realize that although the restoration of life to the dead appears impossible when measured against the capacities of man, it is something straightforward when measured against the infinite power of God Who first inhaled life in the inanimate form of man.

Man may well ask himself how the breath of life may be

inhaled anew into the particles of his body once they have been scattered in the recesses of the earth, and how lifeless matter may be brought back to life although its constituent elements have been dispersed.

But that dispersal does not result in their permanent alienation from each other, and the human intellect can well understand that the infinite and eternal creative power of God has no difficulty in compounding anew those scattered elements so that they begin pulsating with life anew.

The Noble Qur'ān reminds man of God's unlimited ability to restore all the minute qualities and precise details of man's limbs with the following words: "*Does man imagine that We are not capable of reassembling his decayed bones? We are able even to restore his fingers to their previous state*" (75:3-4).

This verse stresses that God is able not only to reassemble the bones of the dead and restore them to life but even, through His boundless and incomparable might, to gather together the scattered particles of their beings and resurrect them.

When the power of God begins to restore to life the order of man's being, in order to implement the ultimate purpose of all being, His infinite power encounters no difficulty in bringing back even the detailed physical characteristics of man, in just the same way that He effortlessly caused the rays of life first to shine on the vast and as yet inanimate plain of being.

In the verse that we have just cited God selects for mention out of all the marvels of man's composition the lines in his fingers as an example of His power. This is significant, because it is possible that individuals should roughly resemble each other with respect to their other limbs, but in the whole world two people cannot be found with exactly identical fingerprints.

Sensory and empirical awareness teaches us that throughout all the changes we undergo in life and all the quantitative transformations to which our bodily composition is subject, the lines in our fingers remain stable and unchanging. This is completely at variance with the continuous changes that occur in our bodily condition.

If the skin on our hands is removed, for some accidental reason, a new skin grows in its place with exactly the same features. Those who specialise in these matters know that fingerprints are therefore the best means for establishing the identity of a person. Throughout the world police have recourse to fingerprints as the surest way for establishing the identity of the author of a crime. This unique quality of fingerprints, first indicated in the Qur'ān, remained otherwise unknown until discovered in 1884 by some British scientists.

Anyone whose mind is oriented to truth and reality will understand, without any hesitation, that the powerful hand of God is at work in the appearance of all these wonders; no intelligent person can accept that some blind mechanical force should be capable of creating the precise and miraculous phenomenon that is man.

Lesson Seven
Resurrection Prefigured in This World

We are witnesses to a ceaseless process of motion and change in the world; everywhere we see impressive scenes of the renewal of life. If we step into the garden in winter, we are confronted with a realm of lifelessness that can be compared, perhaps, to the silent and motionless cemetery where the dead rest. It remains silent and mournful, without the least sign of greenery, vegetation or freshness, until the arrival of spring produces anew the conditions of life and the trees resume their growth and activity. Conditions change all of a sudden once the breeze of life begins to blow over the dead. The soil comes back to life and begins acting anew. On the naked and withered forms of dry, leafless trees new boughs begin to stretch forth, and the earth that had seemingly lost all property of life becomes submerged in fresh flowers and foliage. A pleasing and happy scene takes the place of the cold, dry and spiritless atmosphere of winter.

Such scenes of death and renewal which take place before our eyes every year remain unnoticed by many people. They pass them by with indifference, without their curiosity being aroused and without learning any lesson or making any deduction from this instructive phenomenon.

The power of observation in man needs to grow and develop, just like his capacity for clear thought. It can serve as the source for his understanding of complex matters, but man's tendency to disregard objective realities in his daily life greatly increases his alienation from the truths that surround him and renders barren his mental activity. Careful observation of the changes and transformations that occur in created phenomena and an analysis of the principles of which such changes are based, whether simple or complex, not only helps man to understand the world but also enables him to evaluate his own accomplishments and benefit more from them more fully.

There are many scholars who when confronted with these scenes of death and renewal are led by their intelligence to connect them with the life and death of man; it is as if the concept of resurrection takes on form before the eye of their intellect.

However, we should not imagine that it is only learned scholars who have the capacity to observe and classify objective facts, linking them together in order to reach a conclusion. Despite the varying degrees of knowledge and awareness that men have, the path of reflection and thought lies open for everyone. In proportion to his intellectual capacities, everyone can learn a useful lesson from observing the occurrences and phenomena that surround him.

If dry soil and the naked trees which temporarily suspended their activity because of unsuitable circumstances so that no sign of life was visible in them now abound again in freshness and vitality because of the effect of natural factors such as the generous rainfall, why should we regard the law of the alternation of life and death as being restricted to the vegetable realm? Is there are any reason for denying man a similar resurrection or proclaiming it impossible?

Plants are in fact the best witnesses to the inter- relation of life and death. Within their apparently dead and lifeless seeds are living cells that lie sleeping and sometimes remain healthy and capable of being sown even after thousands of years. After the seeds are planted, the cells awaken to life through the activity of warmth and moisture and begin to grow; flowers, bushes, and grasses begin to emerge from the womb of the earth.

After their deaths, men are buried in that same womb and

are even transformed into earth. Then, when the spring of resurrection arrives and conditions are ripe for the renewal of life, the particles of their bodies begin to stir and they grow forth, just like plants from the seed.

It is true that the generative activity of the earth only apparently ceases with the onset of winter because of natural causes; there is no real death or complete cessation of life. But what is certain that a stagnation takes place, a cessation of vital activity. We must remember, moreover, that when life was first created the whole planet was empty of living beings, only when the environment became favorable did the first spark of life leap forth from the earth.

Life, a Mysterious Truth

Life is indeed a mysterious truth. It may be preserved, sleeping and motionless, in dry genes and atoms for thousands of years, and then, as soon as the environmental conditions become favorable, emerge from the atoms and cells that have become dust and begin growing. There is no scientific reason for rejecting such a hypothesis.

Researchers have discovered life in viruses that cannot be seen even with the aid of electronic microscopes that enlarge objects millions of times; despite their invisibility even to such sophisticated devices, they have the capacity of life, motion and reproduction.

Although man is able to investigate life in such infinitesimally small worlds, he can never exhaust all forms of life. He has not yet been able to establish the exact dimensions of the genes and the chromosomes be means of which he has inherited the attributes and characteristics of his parents and ancestors. Despite this, life emerges from precisely these relatively low organisms that border on the atom.

If life can take up residence within such invisible particles, safe from all hostile forces, in such a way that no type of change is able to expel it from its refuge and destroy it, what reason is there to think that it could not be preserved over a drawnout period in the cells of the human body that have been turned into earth? Or, to use another comparison, why should those cells not come back to life like insects that sleep through the winter? In short, is there any obstacle at all to life ultimately re-emerging from death?

The Qur'ān, which encompasses in its gaze the whole vast and moving arena of life and death, compares man's restoration to life with the resurrection of the plants:

"Thus We bring back to life the dead earth, and the coming back to life of the dead on the day of resurrection shall be similar" (50:11).

Or, in another verse:

"God brings you forth from the ground like the plants and He will then cause you to return to the earth. Then He will bring you forth once again from the earth" (71:17-18).

In these verses, God provides those who do not believe in the hereafter with proofs taken from the sensory and material life of the world (in which, of course, they do believe) in order to demonstrate to them the reality of a future life. He answers the unbelievers with clear evidence taken from the miraculous book of nature. Nonetheless, foolish and obstinate people disregard the instructive phenomena that surround them and close the windows of their heart on the truth.

Let us listen again to the summons of the Qur'ān:

"Look at the dry, barren earth and see how life emerges in it when We send rain upon it. Plants spring forth of every type. This is an indication that God speaks the truth and will revive the dead; certainly He is capable of all things" (22:5).

When the rain pours down and water penetrates the depths of the soil, the air that is concentrated there is pushed downward, causing a ferment within the soil.

When the roots of plants grow within the soil they appropriate part of the soil and their volume increases several times over, so that the earth itself swells and expands considerably through the growth of the plants it contains.

The Commander of the Faithful, 'Alī b. Abī Ṭālib, peace be upon him, said: "I am astonished by the one who denies resurrection in the hereafter although he cannot fail to see it in this world."[16]

The Imām expresses in these words his amazement at those negligent ones who are indifferent to phenomena that are fraught with meaning.

Possessing an effectiveness that extends across time, the Noble Qur'ān should be used as a key to unlock the mysteries of the universe. When discussing the creation of the foetus it again draws man's attention to resurrection in the following words:

"O mankind, if you doubt the day of resurrection and the ability of God to restore life to the dead, know that We have created you from dust, then from a drop of sperm, then from coagulated blood, and then from a lump of flesh, partly formed and partly unformed, demonstrating Our power through all of these changes. We appoint a certain time for what lies in the womb, and then We bring you forth from the womb in the shape of an infant, so that you may live and grow to maturity. Some of you die during this process and others of you reach old age and the time of weakness and impotence even to the extent of losing your understanding" (22:4).

"Man must reflect on the materials from which he was created. He was created from a drop of gushing sperm that issues from between the loins and the ribs. God Who is thus able to create man from this insignificant liquid is without doubt capable of reviving him after his death" (89:5-8).

In connection with the resurrection of decomposed bodies, the Qur'ān discusses the question of motion and change. It points out that just as God Almighty, at the beginning of creation, fashioned man out of particles of clay and then set him on the earth, in accordance with precise laws of His own devising, He will also restore man's bodily frame in its precise, original form, in accordance with another set of carefully planned changes.

For He is all-knowing and well aware of all forms of creation and origination. He knows the course of development on which the decayed body and bones of man must be placed in order for them to recapture their original form. Like all divine acts, this too will take place in accordance with universal norms.

If re-creation is impossible, we must dismiss as impossible not only resurrection and the hereafter but also the initial creation of man through the transformation of particles of dust into his physical form.

We know that man is nurtured by means of various foodstuffs; the compressed essences of earthly substances — fruit, vegetables, meat and dairy products — have a primary role in assuring his physical needs.

It can be said then that the drop of sperm which passes through various stages of development ultimately takes on the form of a man is itself a form of the earth that has undergone change; it results in a newborn infant which possesses a special rank and loftiness among all the phenomena of creation, by virtue of the pure qualities that are inherent in it.

If we reflect on the transformation of lifeless clay first into a drop of sperm and then into a human being, this will clarify for us the question of resurrection and the restoraton of life to the dead.

The verses just cited draw the attention of man in the first place to the beginning of creation and the material out of which his being was fashioned so that he might reflect on the stages he traversed before becoming a fully formed human being. They then raise the question of whether so powerful a planner and designer could be incapable of gathering together the scattered particles of man's physical being in order to fashion them into a new form and inhale in it anew the spirit of life.

The Qur'ān has recourse here to a rational analogy: if an individual or group of individuals is able to perform a certain deed, it follows that they are capable of performing another deed of the same type or even one better than it.

Here, however, we are not dealing with a greater or more complex task. The argument relates rather to one that is simpler and more straightforward: after the collapse of the compounds of which the body is made up, God wishes to re-create man out of existing materials.

We thus come to understand clearly the truth of these

divine words: "*We created you from earth and We will return you to earth, and then bring you forth again from earth*" (20:55).

The Development of the Foetus

The consecutive developments that the foetus undergoes in its own world, its passage through a remarkable series of transitional stages as it pushes forward, is one of the most remarkable phenomena in the whole of the created world.

Man is completely unable to affect its passage through these various stages, which takes place under the control of forces internal to the body and is able at all times to surmount all obstacles successfully.

The cells of the foetus resemble each other during various stages of growth and no sign can be found in the mass of cells of man's different limbs. The circumstances under which abrupt changes take place in identical cells permitting the formation of the limbs of the body is entirely unknown.

After reposing for a time in a temporary resting place, the intermingled cells separate from each other and each of them makes its way to the limb for which it is destined. The form of the foetus is composed of these cells and it gradually begins to take shape.

Then God's power inhales the spirit of life into this inanimate form, enabling a precious entity to emerge on to the plain of existence.

Alexis Carrel, the celebrated French thinker, writes as follows concerning the miracle that the cells of the foetus represent:

"We know that human body is first formed out of a single cell. As the foetus develops, this single cell is transformed into two cells, each of which is then divided into two other cells. This process of division continues until the foetus has completed its growth.

"Although the structure of the foetus becomes progressively more complex with each instant of its growth, it retains the simplicity of function that marked its original seed. Even when they have become a countless mass, in proportion to the growth of the limbs, the cells retain the memory of their original unity, and they know in advance the functions they are to assume in the total scheme of the body.

"The construction of each limb takes place in accordance with a particular method, in the most remarkable way. The materials that are represented by the cells are not put together like the building materials needed to construct a house, and in fact we cannot speak here of a 'construction' taking place, in the strict sense of the word. It is true that just as a house is fashioned of bricks, the body is built out of cells. But in order for the two procedures to be comparable, we have to suppose a house built from a single brick. The brick in question would have to be capable of yielding numerous additional bricks, through the use of river water, mineral salts, and gases found in the air. Further, it would have to place those bricks one on top of the other and build walls without the benefit of an architect's plan or the presence of a builder. Then it would have to change the bricks into glass for the windows, plaster for the ceiling, coal for the heater, and water for the bathroom and kitchen.

"In short, the construction of a single limb resembles a fairy tale of the type told to children."[17]

* * * * *

It is truly remarkable that the All-Powerful Creator fashions the symmetrical and well-proportioned form of man out of a single cell that appears in the womb. That form contains, moreover, numerous organs and capacities that operate independently and continuously from the moment of their formation in the womb until death.

This being the case, cannot God restore to their original state the particles that have become scattered by death but have nonetheless a single origin of which they are merely the changed form?

Can the one who reflects on the remarkable creation of the foetus persist in regarding the restoration of life to the dead as impossible? Does the resurrection of the dead represent something loftier and more difficult? In order to grasp the truth, we must not assess things in a limited, defective fashion. We must reflect instead on the miraculous realities that preside over the universe.

* * * * *

In the animal kingdom the replacement of defective organs and limbs recurs constantly. Certain reptiles, for example, are able to reconstruct a limb or part of a limb when they lose it. There is a kind of worm which can be cut up into numerous pieces, and then each piece becomes a complete worm.[18]

Although man is incapable of this kind of repair work, we should not regard it as impossible that given the right conditions and a suitable environment, the whole body of man should grow anew from a single particle, just like a tree growing from a branch that has been grafted on another tree. This is demonstrated by the fact that in the favorable environment provided by the womb a human being is fashioned from a single cell.

To put it differently, in the same way that the seed of a flower holds within the secrets of all flowers and in the environment that is suitable for its growth develops into a beautiful rosebush which scatters its perfume, so too a single cell can preserve in itself all the characteristics of a fully developed human being and re-create them in a suitable environment.

Someone asked Imām al-Ṣādiq, upon whom be peace.

"Does a corpse decay?"

He answered: "Yes, to such a degree that not a single trace remains of the flesh or the bones. The only thing that does not decay is the earth out of which it was created. It moves about freely in the tomb until it is created anew, as it was the first time."[19]

What the Imām meant by free motion in the tomb was probably the activity of the atoms of the body, for electrons revolve constantly around their central core. After the cells die and the body rots in the grave, the atoms that once composed the body persist and are preserved in an unending circular motion.

Once again the Glorious Qur'ān sets forth, in the clearest possible way, the limitless power of God and invites the deniers of the truth to reflect on the nature of their own existence. The Qur'ān regards the question of resurrection as perfectly comprehensible for those who examine all things in the light of intelligence. It proclaims: "*Does man imagine that he has been left to his own devices? Was he not a drop of sperm that was then changed into a clot of blood and then created in his present form, as a male or female infant? Cannot so wise and powerful a Creator restore life to him after his death?*" (75:36-40).

Miraculous Dimensions of Existence

A profound scientific examination of the totality of the world and the numerous miracles that are enclosed within its horizons is capable — once combined with faith in the boundlessness of God's power — of convincing man fully of the principle of resurrection and of setting his mind entirely at rest. This is particularly the case when we also take into consideration the limits that have been placed on man's knowledge and awareness. If we try to comprehend all the various dimensions of existence, the relative paucity and inadequacy of man's knowledge becomes fully apparent. Scientists themselves know full well that the achievements of science, for all the progress that has been made, will never be able to provide answers for all questions.

Man's limited powers of observation and thought become even more unequal to the task of perceiving reality when his spirit is sunk in the mire of obstinacy.

We know how varied are the forms of life that are to be found on this small planet of ours, which in itself counts as nothing once measured against the dizzying dimensions of the whole universe, but the particularities of many of those forms of life are unknown to us. This is in itself a reason why those who reject the possibility of resurrection should not deny it with such ignorant obstinacy; at the very least they should approach the topic in a more cautious and less categorical manner. Careful observation of the realities that exist all around us can acquaint us in some measure with the amazing power of the Creator, permitting us to understand, for example, that resurrection and the restoration of life to the dead is not more difficult or significant than the original creation of the world with all its complicated mechanisms that function in complete harmony with each other. It is thus that matters will be seen by those who have open minds.

The Qur'ān says: "*The creation of the heavens and the earth, together with the various species of animals that are scattered across its surface, is one of the tokens and signs of God's power. He is capable of gathering them all together whenever He wishes and desires, and His power fully suffices to bring about resurrection*" (42:29).

"*The unbelievers swear oathes that God will never bring back to life one who has died, but resurrection is the firm promise of God. However, the majority of mankind are unaware*" (16:38).

"*The unbelievers imagined that they would never be resurrected. O Messenger, say to them: I swear by my God that you will certainly be resurrected and be made aware of the consequences of your deeds*" (64:7).

"*Is God who created the heavens and the earth in this fashion without becoming weakened or tired unable to resurrect the dead? Certainly God has the power to do all things*" (46:33).

In short, the One Who with the hand of His power created the total scheme of being with all the miracles it contains, Who has caused His eternal and inviolable justice prevail over all things, whether great or small, and Who has bestowed life on a part of His creation – such a One is definitely able to restore life to the dead. Such restoration of life will certainly be easier than the first creation of the entire universe, for any intelligent person will grant that it is far simpler to reassemble the scattered components of a single being than it is to summon the whole of creation into existence.

Is it more difficult to assemble a piece of machinery or to make it? There can be no doubt that it must be easier for the maker or inventor of a piece of machinery to disassemble its parts and then put them back together again.

This leads us to the observation that God as the Creator is the inventor of man. First He created him out of a handful of earth and then He gave life to successive generations of men by means of a single cell. Without doubt He will not face any obstacle when He wishes to gather the scattered particles of man's being and join them together again.

Just as God transforms an invisible cell by means of a well-ordered plan into billions of cells, and then into bones, skin and flesh, thereby bringing into existence a perfect human form, He is also able to repeat this process by causing the atoms that have undergone change to grow again and receive life anew.

All that impinges on our awareness in the creation of an individual is that one person is born of another, but God is aware of all aspects of creation.

Thus the Qur'ān declares: "*He has knowledge of every kind of creation*" (36:79).

For He has the infinite power that was required to create the first living being out of a handful of earth, without any process of birth taking place.

In analysing these truths, the Qur'ān proclaims:

"*Have you not perceived that you were first a drop of sperm? Was it you who created that drop of sperm in the form of a human child or was it Us? We have decreed death for all Our creation. If We wished, We could destroy all of you and replace you with a new creation, or raise you up in a way of which you are now unaware. You are aware of the first creation; why do you pay no heed to the second creation?*" (56:57-62).

Mention is made in these verses of the divine will that has caused man to pass through various stages of growth before attaining his full development. It is stressed that all of these stages take place in accordance with God's wishes and without man being able to intervene in the slightest. It is He Who brings us into this world, moves us through it, and then removes us from it, without either consulting us or seeking the assistance of anyone.

The limitless will and power that man is compelled to obey through all the stages of his growth and development is certainly able to repeat the whole process.

The Qur'ān declares clearly: "*He is God Who began creation and then restores it to its original form after death and dispersal. This restoring is quite easy for Him*" (30:27).

The Qur'ān reminds men that they should reflect with care on the manner in which their life began and on the powerful hand that conveyed them from their first lowly state to their present high station.

Man's progress from being a drop of sperm to becoming a being of value takes place only through the will and command of God Almighty, for there were epochs in which not even the name of man existed.

The Qur'ān says: "*Did not a time pass over man when he was a thing unmentioned? We created him out of a mingled drop of sperm and We gave him the power of sight and hearing*" (76:1-2).

The existence of man is inexplicable without the existence of an originator, a creator. He has not been cast into the world as the product of a series of unconscious factors, but rather for a certain purpose: to traverse the stages of the path leading to perfection, by means of his own choice and devotion, and to attain his true and absolute object of worship. It was the grace of the wise Creator that caused the rays of the spirit to shine on lowly and worthless matter in order for the form of man to come into being, to enter the world, and finally to return toward Him.

So God is the beginning and origin of man and also his purpose and destination.

All our being and aspiration is Your gift;
all our existence is of Your making.
You displayed to non-being the pleasure of being;
and made non-being enamored of Yourself.
We existed not and we made no demand;
Your generosity heard what we left unsaid.

Lesson Eight
The Autonomy of
the Spirit as a Proof of Resurrection

The existence and independence of the spirit can also be adduced as a decisive and convincing proof of life after death. Numerous theories have been put forward by scholars concerning the riddle of the spirit, and the greater becomes the scope of philosophical enquiry and the more carefully use is made of human knowledge, the clearer and more convincing become the proofs for the existence of the spirit and its independence from the body. Of course, we cannot be completely successful in clarifying the quiddity of the spirit, nor can we can lift the veil from the numerous complex mysteries of this eternal entity.

For this reason, the Qur'ān depicts the essence of the spirit as an unknowable truth the complete cognition of which lies beyond man's reach. When the Prophet, peace and blessings be upon him and his family, was asked concerning the essence of the spirit, the Qur'ān told him to answer as follows:

"*O Prophet, they ask you concerning the nature of the spirit. Tell them: 'The spirit is an affair of God, and its essence is unknowable to man. Whatever understanding of it has been given to you is extremely slight*" (17:85).

Fourteen centuries have passed since the Qur'ān gave this answer. The scope of human knowledge is today very much greater than it was in the time of the Prophet, but very little has been added to this aspect of man's awareness. The essential nature of the spirit still eludes man's grasp, and nobody has been able to clarify it. Just as the Qur'ān proclaimed, it remains veiled in a halo of obscurity, and it is highly probable that it will always remain so.

* * * * *

Henri Bergson, the well-known philosopher, says:

"We can conform to Plato and offer a definition of the spirit that is antecedent to experience. We can say that the spirit, being simple, is indivisible, and that because it is indivisible it is also incorruptible, and that it is therefore eternal in its essence.

"For two millennia men have reflected on this concept of Plato, but it has not advanced our knowledge of the spirit in the slightest."[20]

Dr. Chesser, an English scholar, writes:

"Some people say that the mechanical operations of our brain form the ego or the self. Others say that it consists of the brain with the addition of a mysterious spark which leaves our bodies at the time of death. As you know, the philosophers have reflected a great deal on the spirit: its nature, its locus in the body, whether it is mortal or eternal, but none of these questions has yet been solved, despite the continuing of efforts of scholars.

"Recently many scholars have decided to study the matter from another point of view by putting the whole question of the spirit aside as too complex and obscure and studying instead the mind or the soul — i.e., the totality of man's feelings, beliefs and thoughts."[21]

Indeed, if one takes into consideration the fruitlessness of all efforts undertaken for understanding the spirit, how can he believe that it contains some mysterious property which compels our submission and veneration?

The Noble Qur'ān says the following, in the course of some of its verses concerning the creation of man:

"*We created man out of pure earth, then We made him into a drop of sperm and lodged him in a safe place. Then We made the sperm into coagulated blood, the coagulated blood into a formless piece of flesh, and the flesh into bones, and finally We clothed the bones in flesh. Thus We brought forth a new creation. Glorified be the perfect power of the Best of creators!"* (23:12-14).

"*Then God completed the creation of man and inhaled in him of His own spirit and appointed for you eyes, ears, and a heart. How little you men give thanks!"* (32:9).

"*When I complete the outer creation of man and breathe into him of My own spirit, prostrate yourselves before him, O angels!"* (15:29).

These verses describe the successive stages of creation that succeed the coming into being of the drop of sperm, the final result of which is a perfected human body; they indicate that something more valuable and significant is at issue than the creation of a mere corporeal form. They indicate that the infusion of the spirit into man's bodily form constitutes itself a "new creation," which belongs to a category different from the various stages of the evolution of man's bodily form, each of which is necessarily accompanied by the traces and properties of matter. The spirit is a different essence, bearing no similarity to the things created before it. Infused into man's bodily composition, this spirit which God relates to Himself and is thus the closest of all things to Him is independent of the body and separate from it, beyond the reach of matter and all its attributes and properties.

Even the materialists — despite all the differences of opinion and ideology that separate them from the followers of religion — do not go so far as to deny the existence of something called the spirit. They regard sciences such as psychology and psychiatry as valid, but part company with the theologians and metaphysicians on the existence of a second reality in man that subsists apart from the material body and independently of it; this reality has a nature peculiar to itself and is the source of thought and reflection in man.

This does not mean that body and spirit are two realities that are separate from each other, in the sense of each expressing itself completely independently of the other. They are two realities that are connected to each other while being utterly different in their essences.

Beliefs of the Materialists

The thoughts of the materialists on this topic are based on the assumption that a substance called the spirit does not exist independently of matter. They insist that all the activities of the brain are controlled by the laws of matter and result from physical causes and chemical reactions of the brain cells and nerves.

Our nervous system at all times links our perceptions to a central organ, the brain, and these perceptions in turn give rise to a single and indivisible whole. The phenomena that we associate with the spirit are nothing other than physico-chemical reactions. When the brain cells are exhausted and the reciprocal influence of the bodily organs comes to an end, so that the cells cease motion and reproduction, nothing is left of the essence of man save a material form. It is therefore impossible to accept any kind of spiritual immortality or the existence of an autonomous, independent, supranatural entity in man, for both the first appearance and the subsistence of the "spirit" were caused by a spatially and temporally determined connection.

Here the materialist and religious schools of thought part company decisively.

* * * * *

If we accept the claims of the materialists, man will be like a machine, put together from different components and parts, and all traces of life and thought in him terminate utterly once the reciprocal influence of his material components comes to an end. Such an interpretation of the matter fails to do justice either to the reality of the human spirit or to that of man himself.

It is true that the body submits involuntarily to physiological law, but this observable reality does not lead to the conclusion that man is in his entirety chained to the laws of matter with the force of a mathematical equation. There is certainly a close connection between the phenomena of the spirit and the cells of the brain; without having at its disposition a certain number of instruments and tools, the spirit cannot undertake any activity at all in this world. The brain cells, the nerves, and the chemical reactions of the brain, all count as the tools of the spirit by means of which it accomplishes its activity.

It must be asked whether not only the spirit but also its manifestations such as will, determination, perception and so forth, are realities independent of matter, or are themselves entirely material, dependent upon it in all conditions and circumstances.

By way of analogy it may be asked if we conduct a long-distance conversation by means of the telephone, whether we are the real hearers or the telephone receiver?

Is the telephone simply the instrument by means of which we hear the soundwaves, or is it the true and actual hearer?

Matters are the same with respect to the brain. The brain cells are the tool of the spirit, not its creator. All that the proofs put forward by the materialists establish is that there is indeed a link between man's perceptions and his brain cells, not that the brain itself is engaged in perception. In any event, no theologian maintains that thought takes place outside the sphere of the brain cells.

The effects and necessary attributes of matter must inevitably be found in all material beings; it is unacceptable that the properties of matter should be absent from any material entity. If therefore an entity is lacking in the effects and properties of matter, and the effects and properties it does possess do not coincide with those of matter, there can be no doubt that entity in question is not material.

As an objective reality, man is the source of a series of distinctive effects which inseparably accompany his objective existence. Certain of the realities that prevail in human existence can be explained in terms of material criteria, but others do not accord with the properties of matter and cannot be weighed by its criteria.

Here we encounter the fact that in man, in addition to his material composition, an entity exists that is separate from matter and superior to it; it is the source of various forms of perception that belong to a different category than matter.

In fact, each of the perceptions of man, together with its special properties and attributes, is in itself a clear proof and indication of the existence in man of an entity other than his corporeal composition.

If those perceptions were to be the effect of man's physical makeup, his particular bodily composition, if perception and reflection, hearing and seeing, were simply a function of his nerves, they should be explicable in terms of the laws governing his nervous system and his brain cells. However, they are not.

Let us assume that seeing is the formation of an image in the brain; still the question arises of who sees and perceives, who is the author of the act?

Again, if we assume that man is nothing other than a certain type of material composition in a certain part of which an image has been formed – again we ask whether the one that sees and perceives is the totality of the bodily composition or only that small sector of it in which the image has been formed?

The totality of the material composition cannot see and perceive the image that has been formed in a small part of the whole, and it is also impossible for that part to see and perceive; can a material thing see and perceive the images that are formed in the thing itself? Were it be so, a painting or a piece of paper would be able to see and perceive the paintings that the painter has executed on them.

Although scientists have been able to establish empirically that there is a link between perception and consciousness on the one hand and chemical reactions in the brain on the other hand, the only conclusion they can draw is that the nervous system and the brain play a decisive role in the occurrence of perception and various psychological states. The experiments these scientists carry out do not at all permit the conclusion that the essence of the spirit is equivalent to the activity of these instruments of perception or to physical and chemical effects. Finally, proving that the link exists is in no way sufficient to defining the distinctive states and properties of perception and awareness.

To draw an analogy, the spirit is like the electric power required to set a machine in motion. Whenever the power is cut off, the whole of the machine comes face to face with a kind of death, even though its individual components may be quite sound and unimpaired.

Similarly, when man dies the link between his spirit and his body is severed, but the severance does not mean the destruction and death of the spirit. If our telephone, radio or television stops working, we lose our means of communication, and we no longer hear distant sounds or see distant images. Those sounds and images exist everywhere, but we do not see them or hear them; we become aware of them only when our means of communication is provided by the telephone, radio or television.

Sounds and images subsist, then, independently and separately from the instruments required for their perception. Likewise the spirit of man is independent of the body while being linked to it, and it does not perish with the death of the body.

The Particular Properties of Perception

We know that a basic difference separates the functioning of the brain that of the various parts of the body, all of which have in one sense roughly similar functions. The kidneys, for example, are compounded as a result of various physical and chemical activities; their function is related entirely to the inner organs of man's body. By contrast, the phenomena of the spirit relate to the external world that lies outside our personal existence. It is obvious that external world has no ingress to our personal existence; it is on the contrary we who must attempt to comprehend it in order to become aware of external existents, a task of which our brain cells are incapable. Like other dimensions of our body, the brain cells receive effects from the external world but they cannot gain awareness of the nature of matters in the external world. Were that not the case, we ought to be able to perceive the external world with our stomach and lungs. The special nature of our perceptions tells us, then, that another entity rules over our beings.

Let us raise another question at this point: who is it that judges the images that are formed in our brain?

If we meet two people, one of them old and the other young, and images of both of them are formed in our brain, we compare the two images and decide which person is old and which is young.

Several factors are at issue in this decision. First, the seeing and perceiving of the two images that are formed in the brain. Second, the comparison of the two images and the identity of the person that makes the comparison. With respect to this second point, it may be asked how man acquires the power to compare if he consists of nothing more than a series of bodily compounds. Third, the perception of the old man as being more aged than the young man, which follows on the comparison of the two images; here, the perceiver must also establish a relationship. If man consisted exclusively of his bodily form and lacked any non-material dimension, he would be totally unable to establish such a relationship. For a relationship does not have any sensory shape or form that can express itself as an image; we cannot possibly explain the establishment of a relationship through recourse to the criteria of matter.

The fourth issue is perceiving one of the two men as being older than the other. Again we can say that if man consisted only of his physical being, he would not be able to determine which of the two images that have formed in his mind represented an older person.

When we distinguish truth from falsehood, when we appreciate beauty and separate it from ugliness, we are dealing with matters that are external to us and judging them in accordance with certain criteria. The existence within us of a capacity to distinguish truth from falsehood, right from wrong, to measure phenomena external to us by criteria of our own, demonstrates in itself the independence of the spirit. Judgement and discernment are beyond the capacity of the nervous system; they derive exclusively from the operation of thought and the activity of the mind, and cannot be explained in sensory terms.

The unseen light within our inner beings that permits us to distinguish good from evil, beauty from ugliness, right from wrong, is an absolute reality and is none other than our eternal spirit. All temporal occurrences revolve around it, for it is itself an immutable and indivisible pivot of all things.

One of the precious properties of man is his ability to perceive universals, which permits him, after analyzing his experience and sensory perceptions to deduce permanent, fixed and unchanging universals from the particulars that he has observed.

With his sense of touch, for example, man can feel the weight of iron. After repeating this sensory perception, he engages in analysis and reaches the universal conclusion that iron is heavy.

It is thus that man deduces the universal laws and realities that exist in all the particular instances, by analyzing the particulars and abstracting them form their temporal and spatial contexts. These universals form an important part of man's knowledge, for they are the source for his conclusions and judgements.

Were we to regard man as consisting exclusively of his bodily form and to deny the existence of an autonomous spirit, we could not explain the knowledge of universals in any acceptable way, for we would confront the problem of how the processes of analysis or abstraction to which man's sensory experiences and perceptions are subjected take place.

How could the physical composition of our bodily form undertake the tasks of abstraction and the deduction of universal rules from particular instances?

If we regarded the deduction of universals from particulars as a reactive function of matter, precisely how would it take place? How can we depict, as a material process, the perception of a universal principle?

When we perceive a universal principle, we are in fact perceiving an objective reality that is free of all material, temporal and spatial characteristics; it is the existential effect of an entity superior to matter.

If despite all this, some people wish to insist on a materialistic explanation of the matter, their explanation must count as unrealistic, baseless and far removed from the truth.

The Unity of the Personality

Another matter which can help us to appreciate the autonomy of the spirit is the unity of the human personality which covers the entirety of man's life. There can be no doubt that man's knowledge of himself is different from his knowledge of beings external to himself. His knowledge of those beings occurs by means of a reflection of them being traced in his mind; it is thus that we gain the kind of knowledge that is known as "acquired knowledge."As for the knowledge that man gains of his own self, it does not come about through the occurrence of an image in his mind; it is present with him at all times and is inseparable from him, being known therefore as "present knowledge."

This constant presence, which is not subject to change or diminution, and possesses stability and permanence in its ability to feel and gain awareness, represents the clearest and most evidential form of human knowledge.

The entity which is exempt from change and impermanence (these being the attributes of all external reality), which controls and rules the material body, which is not subject to biological determinism, which expresses itself as "I", – this entity is one and the same from the first stages of life until its last moments. Man enjoys permanence by virtue of the permanence of this entity. Its ontological level is infinitely higher than that of matter and material beings, for the unity of the human personality is preserved throughout all the stages of change an individual undergoes in his lifetime.

Can this unchanging entity in any way be ascribed to or regarded as identical with the brain cells?

The contents of the brain cells completely change during the life of an individual through the absorption of matter external to themselves and the transformation of it into energy. New material takes the place of material that dissolves. In fact, every living creature may be re-created several times over in the course of his life as a result of the ceaseless changes of his molecules and the particles of his body.

Were we to be composed only of matter and were there to be no invisible force controlling the mass of our cells and the structure or our bodies, given the fact that the content of our nervous system and our brains changes several times over in the course of, say, fifty years, and the entirety of our physical form undergoes various fundamental changes, the reality of our being would be entirely controlled by the attributes of matter and we would no longer be the same distinctive person that we were last year. We know, however, that there is a single stable and immutable reality which comprises our personality and assures its unity and distinctiveness.

That stable entity which exists in man is like the reflection of the moon or the sun, shining night and day on the water. Although the waves are in constant motion and flux, one wave advancing to have its place taken by another, the reflection of the light of the moon or the sun is stable and uniform:

Time and again the water has changed in the stream,
But the light of the moon and the stars maintains its gleam.

The stable and immutable spirit keeps shining down on the river of the body, just like the light of the moon and the sun. Although the cells and molecules of the body perish, the slightest change does not occur in the essential personality of man.

Everyone can perceive the existence within himself of a spirit that is both independent of the body and possesses a form of existence totally different from that of the body. Everyone is aware within himself of an identity that is autonomous, continuous, constantly present, and stands in contrast to his material being which changes every day.

One cannot possibly regard an entity that thus dominates the body and unlike the body is immune to diminution as being the product of matter or subordinate to its rules. Any supposition of this type cannot explain anything concerning the true nature of man.

Cressy Morrison writes:

"What is certain is that the creation of this world was not the outcome of accident or chance, because the entire order of the world revolves around specific laws.

"The appearance among the animals of man, endowed with thought and intelligence, is too mysterious and too significant for us to imagine it to be the result of material processes, without the hand of a Creator being involved. If this is not the case man must be like a mechanical instrument requiring someone also to set him to work. But then whose hand would it be that sets him in motion?

"Until now, science has not been able to provide any explanation of who this operator might be, only one thing is certain — that the operator cannot be a material compound.

"We have progressed only so far as to imagine God bestowing a flash of His own knowledge on our existence. Man is still passing through his infancy in the understanding of creation and is just beginning to understand the existence of the spirit; he is gradually becoming aware of this heavenly gift and its eternal, everlasting character."[22]

If the manifestations of the spirit are simply part of the effect and properties of the body, the outcome of the activities of the brain, or reducible to the total functions of the nervous system, how can we analyse and explain the persistence of the human personality?

It is, after all entirely natural to suppose that an entity which refuses to submit to the laws of matter should be permanent and everlasting.

The explanation offered by certain materialists to the effect that the self is relative and that it undergoes change and development while possessing stability, is more of a poetic than a scientific nature; it cannot in any way explain the unity preserved by the human personality throughout life. For this incorrect theory arises from a theory of man which is even more erroneous; it would imply that "I am not now that man that I previously was; I am someone who has taken his place but I somehow fancy that I am the same person as before. In addition, these imaginings are my act and I am their source; it is not that my self comprises the varied and ever-changing concepts that take form in my mind."

Lesson Nine
The Sovereignty of the Spirit

We are aware of two realities in our being: one the external compound that is our body, fully accessible to empirical science, and the other, consisting of thought and perception, love and affection, hatred, and conscience. These cannot be considered as a mere series of sensory needs or bodily reactions; they are beyond the scope of empirical science and cannot be measured by material criteria.

They represent realities that are both different from the material body and superior to it, being capable of dominating it. For example, a person might be ready to die in the course of a hunger strike in order not to suffer the shame of servility at the very same time that biological forces are destroying his body and urging him to surrender and eat. In other circumstances, too, a person may be hungry, but he continues to fast.

Here we have a perfectly concrete and observable case of an iron will sacrificing the body for the sake of an idea, an abstract ideal. This is something that cannot be explained by the logic of materialism.

Those who claim that man is simply a collection of physiological and material functions have to provide a serious and logical explanations of cases such as this. If I am nothing more than my material form, how is it possible that I should command my body and make it obey me?

The answer, of course, is that there is a reality separate

from the body and empowered over it. The fact that the will can issue commands and establish a kind of inner dominion over man's various instincts and bodily aspects is a clear proof for the existence in man of a sublime, supramaterial element from which his will draws its power.

The duality of these realities in man, and the dominance exercised by one of them over the other, points us to the existence of something higher than matter.

The Noble Qur'ān proclaims: "*By the soul and the One Who created it in perfection and inspired in it knowledge of good and evil deeds*" (91:7-8).

This means that man has been adorned with an essence which possesses perception and motion: it has perception because it has received inspiration, and it has motion because it is the origin of a series of deeds oriented either to piety and virtue or to corruption.

What is this essence that is qualified by awareness and ability?

None of the parts of man's earthly body possess these properties. There must therefore be an essence which is autonomous and separate from the body and yet accompanies it while possessing the attributes just mentioned.

Matter reacts in a uniform and predictable way to external stimuli. Water solidifies when confronted with extreme cold; metals expand when confronted with extreme heat – these reactions are natural and unchanging. But man is capable of manifesting the most varied and even contradictory reactions, and this is in itself a proof that the powerful spirit and will of man are non-material, for they transcend the properties of matter.

* * * * *

The process whereby perception takes place shows that there are two factors involved: the means of perception (the eye, for example) and the faculty of perception. It is a law of physics that you can never perceive a motion while you are yourself a part of that motion; the motion can be perceived only outside itself.

It is possible for you to perceive a moving object only when you stand, as it were, on a platform that is outside the sphere of the motion. This enables you to see the passage of things in front of you and to sense the motion of time. It is not possible for man to sit down on the ground and measure the rotation of the earth, nor can he stand on the moon and measure its rotation. Motion is visible only from outside itself.

So if our faculty of perception were not located outside the range of unceasing motion, we would never be able to perceive motion and the passage of time; the fact that we are able to perceive the passage of time is a clear proof that our faculty of perception is beyond the reach of time.

If, for example, our faculty of perception were to change and to move each instant, in keeping with the perpetual motion of time, we would be unable to perceive the passage of time, for our faculty of perception would be shattered into disconnected fragments.

So since we perceive time, our faculty of perception must exist outside the scope of time and transcend it.

This distinguishes our faculty of perception from our bodily form, and it might be said, indeed, that one half of the reality of man becomes worn out, old and exhausted, while the other half escapes dissolution in the whirlpool of time and pursues its own life.

The Commander of the Faithful, peace be upon him, said:

"O people, we have been created to live eternally, not to perish. However, you will change your place of residence, and move forward from one stage to another. Make provision, then, for the world to which you will go after this transient abode and in which you will reside eternally."[23]

The Great Storehouse of Mental Images

The exitence of a specific relationship between a container and a thing contained is one of the properties of matter; a larger thing can never be made to coincide entirely with a smaller one.

If for example we stand on some great elevation, and gaze over the vast plains that surround us, with all their trees, verdure, and birdlife, their hills and their vales, their great rocks piled up on top of each other, and if we then try to picture all these items in our minds, they will appear before our spirit, our inner vision, like a great picture, with all the attributes they possess.

Here we may ask whether all these varied images, with the extensiveness that they possess, both in the external world and in our minds, are stored up in our brains, with their very small and delicate cells?

Does such limited matter have the capacity to accommodate — precisely and without any diminution — so vast a series of images?

Without doubt, reason and logic compel us to answer in the negative, for anyone can understand that it is impossible to make a larger object conform — while retaining its exact quantity — to a smaller one. For is it not the case that the container must either be larger than the object contained or at least equal to it? It is impossible, for example, to typeset on a single small sheet all the contents of a thousand-page book.

We can easily picture in our minds a big city with all of its buildings, streets, parks, cars and other vehicles, and population. But basing ourselves on the principle that "the large cannot be made to conform to the small," we must conclude that such extraordinarily large mental images cannot be accommodated in the minute cells of our brain; for it self-evident that such comformity can take place only when the object contained is equal in size to the container or smaller than it. In addition, our capacity of perception possesses attributes and properties that do not correspond to those of matter, and it cannot therefore be dependent simply on a series of physical relationships that accompany its functioning.

The only conclusion open to us is, then, that in the formation of mental images we possess a dimension of existence that is additional to certain physical and chemical prerequisites, a dimension that possesses, moreover, properties which transcend those of our material form. One of those properties is precisely the ability to accommodate vast images within itself, and another is the ability to preserve and maintain the images that are perceived.

* * * * *

The materialists say: "These images are like a voluminous book stored up in our brain on microfilm; when necessary, the brain displays the contents of the book in reduced form, and if man wishes to obtain the true dimensions of the object in question, he magnifies the images to restore to them their true size. It is the reduced images that are present in the brain cells."

However, one question remains: where – in the brain or the nervous system – do these magnified images come into being? Either one must negate the possibility of these large images occurring in the mind or one must find a suitable location for them there. Now no one can deny the existence of those images, and if what we call "the spirit" be purely material, with perception being synonymous to the activity of the brain and the nervous system, it is impossible for the small cells of the brain to accommodate such large images. They would need a location proportionate to their size, while all the microfilm is capable of doing is to accommodate small, reduced images.

In order to clarify the whole matter, one must therefore accept the existence of an element not susceptible to sense observation. It is this non-material entity that is capable of creating and observing large mental images, after the brain and the nervous system have accomplished certain preliminary functions. Once we accept this, the whole problem is solved and we have no need to resort to inadequate explanations.

Furthermore, when we compare mental to material phenomena, we must acknowledge that a significant difference exists between them; they have not the slightest resemblance to each other with respect to properties and qualities.

Matter is constantly accompanied by a series of general properties such as the assumption of different forms, something which is not true of mental images. This disparity of mental and material phenomena is another indication of the autonomy and non-material nature of the spirit.

The Bed of Memory

Another aspect of material existents is their subjection to gradual change within time and space, for anything subject to development and gradual change necessarily requires a certain space, and motion in itself creates time. The ineluctable fate of all material existents is therefore to waste away and perish in the course of time.

Again, it is not possible to think of a single material existent that is not capable of division into constituent parts, whether that division takes place by means of special instruments or by means of some other cause.

None of this holds true of the phenomena of the spirit.

We build vast structures in our minds without needing time. All kinds of faces, forms, colors, names, numbers, words, and indications are stored up in the storehouse of our minds without being confused with each other and without encroaching on each other.

The mind perceives and records all kinds of scenes and images, all kinds of events, great and small; it then records them and places them in its archive. Even things that we sometimes think we have forgotten are not in fact erased from our minds; they remain in place and come again to the fore through the action of certain factors.

What secret archive is hidden in the brain capable of storing all these figures, inscriptions and images, in such a way that they do not mingle with each other and can instantaneously leap forth in the mind like a flash of lightning?

Where is the reservoir of these mental images, which are like a bewildering riddle? Is the materialistic interpretation realistic; does it do justice to the facts of the matter? Are our memories material accidents, impressions made on our brain cells? Do the cells and arteries of the brain record events and occurrences, and when we remember something, does the mind simply hand over, carefully and faithfully, the images that it stores?

The Materialist Interpretation Contradicts Reality

When we perceive a certain image we compare it with images previously perceived and then judge whether or not it is identical to them. When we are engaged in this, is not some reality at work as other than the material reality of our body? How can the brain cells undertask the task of comparison? How can they decide that two images are identical, that the second one seen is the same as the first? If we locate judgement in the brain, how can we understand the matter correctly?

Were the brain to be the true location of memory, the memories that are dependent on the brain cells would disappear as the cells themselves decay and their content vanishes.

The material that makes up our brain cells changes numerous times in the course of a single lifetime, but the faces of friends and acquaintances from our childhood remain intact and unchanged in the storehouse of our mind.

If all the contents of our brain were to be changed, including knowledge acquired in the past, in conjunction with the replacement of old brain cells by new, all access to past knowledge would be impossible. New perceptions could only be similar to past perceptions, not identical with them, whereas our perceptions of matters previously perceived constitutes only a renewal of memory, not a renewal of knowledge. To put it more generally, if our mental concepts were material in nature, it would be impossible to gain access by way of memory to knowledge previously acquired.

When we memorize a few lines of poetry or a page from a book, how does the memorization occur in our brain cells? By what method can we assume this process to take place? When we forget something we have memorized, is a certain imprint effaced from our brain cells?

If the memory in question is indeed destined to vanish and disappear, how is it that we can recall it by means of careful reflection? If, on the contrary, the imprint left on our brain cells is immune to destruction, why can we not find it in our minds?

How can we explain the fact that after forgetting something we have memorized, we sometimes hear a sentence from the book or a line from the poem in question, and then the remaining sentences or the rest of the poem spring back to mind. If the imprint left by the book or the poem had been completely effaced from the tablet of our brain, how can it suffice to hear part of what we have memorized for the rest to come back to our mind? But, on the other hand, if the imprint left by memory is not effaced and remains secure in its place, what is the meaning of forgetting?

The celebrated scholar Henri Bergson has the following to say:

"When we examine the observations we make it becomes clear to us that physiological explanations of memory are inadequate; we cannot possibly attribute memorization to the brain.

"Our observations also make it plain that it is quite possible to discern the traces of the continuous expansion of memory, beginning from the point at which the memory mobilizes itself to put forth the effort needed for its function at that instant and ending when the memory lays out the past in the mind in imperishable form.

"We can compare the memory to a pyramid; we begin our examination of its functioning at its apex and work our way down to its base. We must be aware that only the apex of the pyramid is located in matter; as soon as we move away from the apex, in the direction of the base, we begin to enter a different realm.

"What is this realm? We can call it that of the reflective or meditative spirit, for we can clearly sense the existence in this world of a subtle essence or spirit that is independent of the body. Given the fact that an important part of the functions of the spirit are independent of the body even in this world, it is definite that the spirit as such must enjoy permanence after death."[24]

No equation can be established between damage to the brain on the one hand and the phenomenon of forgetting on the other hand. If there were such an equation, every lessening or defect in a given memory would bring about a corresponding lessening or defect in the brain cell to which it is connected.

If certain brain cells are damaged, a person begins to experience difficulty in speaking, but his memories are preserved intact. When the brain suffers serious damage as the result of infection, the equilibrium between memory and the brain is disrupted. Once forgetting sets in, it follows a fixed and regular pattern; the patient forgets first the names of his friends and those around him and then, in later stages, the words used to designate various activities.

Here no relationship is to be seen between damage to the brain on the one hand, and the decline over time in clarity and quantity of memory on the other. According to the logic and analysis of the materialists, there ought to be a direct and proportional relationship between the lessening of memory and the damage suffered by the brain.

All of this shows that the brain is only a means and an instrument for the retention of memories, and that the function of the brain with respect to memory is restricted to the transfer of mental images to verbal form. In other words, it establishes a link between the world of the spirit and the world of matter.

In the acquisition of memories and mental images we need therefore something more elevated than our brain cells, which is none other than our spirit, which is non-material, independent of matter, and our thoughts, images, and memories are all governed by its laws.

Professor Gayton (?), says in his book on physiology, which is regarded as a reliable source on the subject:

"The most complex problem that confronts us in our study of awareness, thought, memory and retention is that we do not know the nervous mechanism of a single thought."

The Indivisibility of the Acts of the Spirit

Judgements and affirmations are indivisible. They do not have any location within the cells of the brain, nor can they be divided in either primary or secondary manner. This is because our perceptions and affirmations are dependent on a non-material entity.

For example, when we say that such-and-such a bird is green, the bird itself is certainly divisible, and likewise its greenness with respect to its locus in the bird. But our affirmation of the greenness of the bird is indivisible.

If we regard thought and reflection as the exclusive product of matter, affirmation – together with the other acts of the spirit – ought to be capable of division, whereas we clearly see that this is not the case. The conclusion can therefore be drawn that since one of the functions of the spirit – thought and reflection – does not possess the material attribute of divisibility and is therefore non-material, so too the spirit, the organ from which thought arises, must also necessarily also be non-material. The non-materiality of thought thus serves as an indication of the non-materiality of the spirit.

Materialists are submerged in their illusory deductions and take delight in denying all belief in the existence of supranatural entities. All their arguments for such vital phenomena of life, awareness and perception are based on unprovable hypotheses, and they can, in any event be refuted with firm and convincing arguments.

Theories such as those they advance cannot remove the veil from the mysteries of life, nor can they solve the knotty problems we confront. Empirical science has in fact demonstrated its inability to explain the nature of the phenomena we have been discussing.

The whole philosophical scheme of materialism, with its inability to answer the questions we have raised, ought to be jettisoned just like coins that have lost their currency. As human thought and awareness progress and man frees himself from narrow and monodimensional thinking, materialism will in fact be cast on the refuse heap which is the final destination of all obsolete and discredited beliefs.

Lesson Ten
The Evidence of Experience

Were the phenomenon of the spirit, which is non-material in all
its aspects, to be made the subject of experimentation, so that
its autonomous existence became fully proven, despite its
remoteness from sense perception, it would have a profound
effect in causing men to believe more fully in the spirit. This
would be the case particularly with those who are unable to
understand subtle and complex questions and who are more
inclined to accept empirical scientific data than they are the
truths of philosophy.

* (1) *

Spiritualism, the practice of communicating with the
spirits of the dead, reached its highpoint in the nineteenth
century when it became codified as a science. Numerous
personalities throughout the world have observed the
possibility of such communication, which may be counted as a
living proof for the autonomy and immortality of the spirit.

Divesting themselves of all partiality and prejudice and
impelled by genuinely scientific motives, a number of scholars
have devoted themselves to painstaking research and study in
order to discover the truth of the matter. With their
achievements they have been able to demonstrate that the
existence of the spirit is no longer a theoretical matter but
something clear and straightforward.

Carefully executed experiments have shown that it is

definitely possible to establish communication with the spirits of the dead. One may engage in conversation with them and ask their help in solving difficult problems. It often happens, indeed, that people who are utterly unable to solve the most complex problems confronting them are able to solve them through communication with the spirits of the dead.

Spirits have also been shown to possess the remarkable capacity of raising bodies from ground without the intervention of any material cause or bodily energy.[25]

One of the prominent traits of those who enter a trance to communicate with the dead is that they function both as receivers and as transmitters. It may sometimes happen that while in that state they speak in languages they had never learned. They may also find themselves divulging secrets they were not in a position to know.

Still more remarkable is the fact that mediums are able while in a trance to read and to copy inscriptions on objects contained in sealed boxes, although they are quite illiterate!

In short, mediums engage in such inexplicable acts that we are obliged to follow them into the invisible realm of the spirit in our attempt to find an answer.

All we have mentioned has been proved by experiment and it constitutes a refutation of the claims of the materialists, for if the spirit were simply an effect of matter, a physicochemical property of the brain, it would be impossible to explain all these varied phenomena that have been verified experimentally.

We can escape the impasse to which materialist thought leads only when we admit the existence of a supramaterial force that creates such phenomena, for it is not conceivable that they should be the product of material factors.

Although age is not an important consideration for those who establish communication with spirits, those who enter on this path generally choose mediums from among children to receive messages from spirits. This removes the likelihood of trickery, deceit, and recourse to various contraptions, and thus puts an end to all possible objection.

At the same time, experienced and specialized researchers also take part in the sessions where contact is established with spirits. Repeated and careful experiments are carried out in order to remove any lingering doubts, to clarify all ambiguity, and to dispel any notion of autosuggestion on the part of the participants.

Although we can accept the matter under discussion as an established reality, it is – like many other truths and realities – exploited by those trade is trickery and deceit; they demean and dishonor it. One cannot therefore either trust all who claim to be able to communicate with spirits, or reject them with inappropriate arguments; both courses would be contrary to logic. It is a careful examination of the matter that will lead to a perception of the truth and the ability to distinguish the illusory from the real.

Farīd Wajdī, author of the *Twentieth Century Encyclopaedia*, lists the names of a handful of European and American scientists from among the many thousands that have worked in this field, and cites the clear evidence provided by the objective experiments they carried out. Many of them were sceptical or negative about the possibility of communicating with the spirits of the dead until it was proven to them; in fact they first entered the field with the intention of totally disproving its bases.

If someone had insisted on the possibility of proving scientifically communication with the spirits of the dead, they would have dismissed it unhesitatingly as an absurdity. But when they saw that whatever experiment was undertaken ended up supporting the claims of their opponents, they surrendered and accepted the facts. Earlier scholars had never taken the trouble to test the claims of the spiritualists, they even regarded the idea of conducting experiments on the subject with repugnance.

Farīd Wajdī adds that specialists in the field believe in the principle that the spirit is not annihilated with the death of the body, because they are unable to explain the extraordinary phenomena that take place in their sessions except in terms of activity by the spirits of the dead.

* * * * *

Those who do not have any serious arguments to offer try to explain these experimentally tested realities in terms of the unconscious.

Can we reasonably accuse all the scholars and experts who work in the field of having been straightforwardly duped by the tricks of swindlers and of placing the seal of scientific approval of on a series of delusions? Of affirming the correctness this science without exercising any caution, under the influence of the mediums?

It would be completely irrational and illogical to attribute error to all those scholars.

Alfred Russell Dulles, Darwin's partner in discovering the law of natural selection, declared his view on the matter as follows:

"When I began investigating the mysteries of communication with the spirits of the dead, I was an absolute materialist and denier of the spirit. No trace existed in my mind of non-material entities or a supranatural world. On the contrary, it was my intention to prove by scientific means the incorrectness of all belief in such things. But as I confronted the experiments that had taken place and the realities they had proven, I gradually came to believe in them myself. The reality of the spirit came to have such an effect on me that I came to believe in it firmly before I was able to find any explanation for it in my mind. I can neither turn away from it in denial nor can I find any material cause for it."[26]

Krokis (?) the head of the Royal Academy of Science in England, writes the following in his book entitled *Spiritual Phenomena:*

"Since I do indeed believe in the existence of these phenomena, it would be a kind of fear or literary cowardice if I concealed my testimony from fear of the criticism of mockers who know nothing at all of the subject and are unable to free themselves of their illusions. I will set forth in my book as clearly as I can what I have seen with my own eyes and tested repeatedly through careful experimentation."

From all the experiments that have taken place in sessions for summoning up the spirits of the dead and the conclusions scholars have drawn from them, it is plain that man possesses an energy and personality that outlive his death. That energy undertakes various activities without any need of the physical body. Under certain special circumstances it is possible for the inhabitants of this world to establish communication with the spirits of the departed.

* (2) *

Another scientific advance that has contributed to the understanding of the autonomy and immortality of the spirit is hypnotism. This consists of concentrating the gaze for a lengthy period of a point of light to the accompaniment of prolonged suggestion, with the result that the subject enters an artificial dream state, quite distinct from ordinary dreams.

After the subject has fallen asleep, he hears out of all sounds that surround him only those produced by the hypnotist all of whose commands he obeys in his extreme impressionability.

The English scholar James Breed (?) was able to build on the investigations of his predecessors to turn hypnotism into a fully fledged science by clarifying the principles according to which hypnotism functions.

After him other scholars in America and Europe devoted their efforts to further developing this science; we can mention in particular Richet, Emile Kue, Van Ouls and Charcot (?). The most important achievement of the last of these was his classification of the different degrees and stages of hypnotic sleep.

"In artificial sleep, the hypnotist is able to make the subject submit to his will in such a way that he unhesitatingly executes his commands. The senses of the sleeper cease functiong; he shows no sign of being able to see or to hear, and his senses of touch and taste lack their customary power. Finally, the one thus put to sleep is so overcome by weariness and lassitude that he feels no pain, however much pressure be brought to bear on his body."[27]

Dr. Philip Carrot, a British anaesthesiologist and specialist on hypnotism, wrote the following in the *British Journal of Public Health*:

"Many patients needing surgery have been successfully anaesthetized through the use of hypnotism." He went on to state his belief that it is easier and better to use hypnotism on patients undergoing surgery, because it is a simpler and less dangerous procedure than drugging them. One of the advantages of hypnotism is that it is possible to keep the patient unconscious for many hours without his feeling any pain.[28]

* (3) *

Magnetism is another branch of knowledge pointing to the autonomy of the spirit. It consists of a mysterious force present in everyone to different degrees. Magnetism differs from hypnotism in that when a person cultivates the magnetic force within him he will be able to influence animals as well as human beings. In addition, magnetic force can be exploited directly, whereas hypnotism requires the use of certain means in order to become effective. The power of magnetism is so effective in man that it enables one to render one's prey or enemy motionless.

Since the most ancient times, people have been aware to some extent of the effects of this mysterious power. It was however at the end of the eighteenth century that it was put forward for the first time as a scientific discovery. Specialists began to use magnetic waves as a means for curing the sick, and as research progressed, it became apparent that hypnotic trances might be induced by means of magnetism.

Psychiatrists make use of artificially induced dreams to discover the causes for certain psychiatric disorders; they attempt to plunge into the depths of the mind and to discover the true thoughts of the unconscious, the thoughts that the patient would be reluctant to tell the doctor while in a waking state, out of embarrassment or other reasons. Likewise, the patient frankly confesses to certain things that he would never reveal while in a waking state.

The one sent into a trance is so fully subject to the influence of the magnetic force that he does whatever he is told by the one who puts him in the trance, without his own will having the least power to decide.

At more advanced stages, the body itself becomes totally numb, and if one of its limbs is rubbed it will be unable to move, resembling an entirely motionless body. The subject will be unable to hear sounds surrounding him; he sees and hears only the one in whose power he stands.

This passivity sometimes goes so far that he feels the pain of a needle inserted in by the one who controls his trance; and likewise if the controller begins to feel happy, so too will the subject! Other emotions — anger, nervousness, excitement — will be similarly reflected.

Persons in a magnetic trance are able to speak in languages they have not learned; they know of things that lie beyond the range of their knowledge; and their spirits travel to distant regions. Materialists attempt to explain all this in terms of suggestion and the loss of customary will on the part of the subject. However, their explanations are not convincing. For in addition to that which the material sciences attempt to explain there is a reality within man capable of accomplishing acts that are inexplicable in terms of material criteria. Anyone who tries to discover the truth of the matter will be led to accept this conclusion, step by step.[29]

What energy is it that can thus subdue the will of another person and rob his limbs of motion and feeling?

If man reflects carefully, will he not be convinced that his existence includes a spirit that is both mysterious and eternal? [30]

Is it not the method of science to base general laws on objective observations and to strive against delusion?

Without any doubt, every new discovery in the fields

discussed above decreases still further any appeal the materialistic distorters of reality might have.

∗ (4) ∗

Although men have been aware of telepathy – at least to some degree – for a long time, no careful scientific study of the subject was undertaken before 1882. Beginning with that date, the English Society for Psychic Research has carried out numerous experiments and proven the reality of the phenomenon.

The communication of thoughts between two people is possible over both long and short distances. Communication over short distances takes place by means of the two people standing opposite each other and transmitting their thoughts to each other without speaking or making any gestures.

As for communication over a long distance – and the size of the distance is of no importance at all – it is enough for the two persons, at a prearranged time, to concentrate their thoughts on a single point in order to transmit their mental messages to each other.

These phenomena have been repeatedly tested and proven by specialists and they can be regarded as another remarkable manifestation of the spirit, acting in utter independence of the body.

Ought we not then to believe that the energy ruling over the mechanism of our body is fundamentally different from material energy and the phenomena it produces? As the psychiatrist Kennington puts it, "for the brain to exist and function a few centimeters outside the body is just as impossible as it would be for digestion or the circulation of the blood to take place outside the body."

Henri Bergson writes: "The phenomena declared to exist by psychic science, at least some of which must be regarded as true, cause us to ask why we have waited so long to undertake such a study.

"We will not repeat the subjects we have already discussed, but instead restrict our discussion to a point that appears more certain than anything else. If after the accumulation of thousands of testimonies consistent with each other concerning manifestations of telepathy scientists still insist on denying the reality of this phenomenon, then we can only conclude that human testimony is unacceptable to science and rejected by it.

"It is true of course that we have to choose among the various results that psychic science presents to us; that science itself does not regard all its results as equally conclusive; and that it distinguishes between what is certain and what is merely probable or possible.

"But if we take into consideration only that part which psychic science regards as definite, it suffices to give us a sense of a vast and unknown realm that psychic science has only just begun to explore."[31]

Lesson Eleven
The Evidence of Experience, (Continued)

Man's ever-increasing curiosity first began to exercize itself on objects that were far removed from him – the stars. Now it is his normal and natural states and circumstances that preoccupy him as he attempts to make out the factors which dominate his existence.

One of the topics that has attracted man's attention is that of sleep and dreams. This is understandable, considering the fact that a significant part of man's life is spent asleep in the world of dreams.

The various theories that have been put forth on this subject demonstrate the complexity of the subject and reflect all the lengthy experiments experts have conducted.

It is a characteristic of man like all living beings to sleep after engaging in effort and tiring activity. As a portion of his vital activity is suspended, the functioning of the body also decreases.

How sleep takes place is itself an important question; despite all the studies that have been made, a definitive answer cannot yet be given. The whole matter is shrouded in a variety of interpretations many of which are the result of hasty and unjustified deductions. All that science knows so far is restricted to certain physical processes which take place in the realm of the body.

There are as yet no indications that permit us to hope for a solution to this problem and it would be incautious to predict the emergence of precise and realistic theories. Nonetheless, the advance of human knowledge may one day enable man to solve this great mystery that confronts him.

Still more mysterious than sleep are dreams – that configuration of various scenes, images and events in the mind of the sleeper. The phenomenon of the dream confronts us with all kinds of complex and knotty problems.

All the physiological functions of the body, all its non-volitional and reflexive acts, continue during sleep with the utmost regularity. The nerves and the glands, the intestines and the muscles all continue their work. But man has no power of thought or decision; his will is inoperative, and his life resembles that of a monocellular being.

The sleeper looks like a lifeless and prostrate figure, but suddenly he awakens and comes back to life. Sleep and awakening are in fact comparable to death and resurrection. The Noble Qur'ān says the following concerning the affinity between sleep and death on the one hand, and awakening and resurrection on the other:

"God takes men's souls at the time of their death, and the soul which does not die He takes in its sleep. Then He keeps the soul that is destined to die at that time, and returns the others to life for a set period" (39:42).

In the view of the Qur'ān, sleep is outwardly the suspension of the natural forces in man, but it is at the same time a return of man's spirit to his inner being. Sleep is the lesser death, and death is the greater sleep. In both cases the spirit is transferred to a different world. The difference is that on waking up a person is unaware that he has returned from a journey, whereas for the one who dies all things become clear.

Dreams have been divided into several categories. A large proportion of dreams derive from the hopes and desires of the dreamer, or reflect occurrences he has experienced.

Another major category consists of confused dreams that simply reflect man's imaginings and illusions.

Then there is a category of dreams of which the defining element is a kind of inspiration; these dreams foretell events. They sometimes reflect an as yet hidden occurrence in its exact and real form and sometimes in symbolic form that can be interpreted by those having the necessary skill.

Since the human spirit has an affinity with the supranatural realm, it is bound to depart for that expansive universe once sleep puts an end to its preoccupation with sensory perceptions. There it witnesses certain realities, in accordance with its degree of preparedness and capacity, and it is able to deposit the knowledge thus received in the mind in a way that permits it to be remembered after the sleeper awakens.

* * * * *

There can be no doubt that confused dreams are connected to certain physical and psychological conditions; they are nothing but a series of illusions and imaginings. Similarly, the appearance in the mind of the dreamer of past events, without any reflection of events yet to come, has no particular value.

This, however, is not the case with dreams the interpretation of which permits one to forecast events that are still in gestation or which, being so clear as to leave no need for interpretation, present to us in the imaginal world the causes and occasions of things in their actual form.

Many instances of this kind of dream have been reported in historical sources. They occur, moreover, in the personal lives of many of us, and they cannot all be ascribed to coincidence. They cannot be attributed either to the reminders of past events of the day or to analyses of them that our nervous system provides us with, nor do repressed instincts and desires play any role in them.

Freud interprets dreams as follows:

"Generally speaking, what appears to us in the world of dreams consists of the sensory objects of which we have been aware during the day and of wishes which have remained unfulfilled for one reason or another. During the day a man may conceive a desire for a certain woman who is inaccessible to him; at night he gains possession of her in the world of his dreams. A hungry beggar dreams of riches and palaces; an ugly man acquires unparalleled beauty; an impotent old man recovers the vigor of youth; a hopeless and desperate man finds all his wishes fulfilled. In short, all the wishes and inclinations that remain unfulfilled during the day, all the feelings that remain hidden for one reason or another, come into the open and are freely satisfied in the world of dreams."

* * * * *

Here I will refrain from mentioning the numerous dreams foretelling the future which are mentioned in historical sources or have been experienced and related to me by countless trustworthy persons. Let me simply recount a dream I had myself. On Saturday, April 24, 1962, a violent earthquake shook the city of Lar, leading to heavy losses of life and damage.

About one week before the earthquake, I dreamed that a strong earthquake was shaking Lar, destroying buildings and raising up clouds of dust that covered the sky like thick fog.

With this terrifying picture pressing on my mind, I woke up in terror, probably at about midnight.

The next day I told some of the notables of Lar and my friends of my dream, and they still sometimes recall the occasion.

At the time, they naturally interpreted my dream in different ways, but two or three nights later an earthquake of medium force occurred, causing only moderate losses. One of the religious scholars of the city came to see me and said: "Yesterday's earthquake is the one that you dreamed of." I replied that the brief and relatively harmless earthquake we had just experienced bore no resemblance to the horrifying scenes I had witnessed in my dream. (The person in question still remembers what happened.)

Finally April 24 arrived. Toward the end of the day a ruinous earthquake was visited on Lar. The city shook violently, buildings collapsed, clouds of earth and dust rose into the air, and countless people, young and old, men and women, were swallowed up by death.

Those who survived the earthquake rushed to the ruined buildings to help the wounded. The sight that presented itself during those grim moments was truly shattering.

A particularly remarkable detail is that in my dream I had seen the small child of one of my relatives who lived in a neighboring house. I saw him passing in front of a part of the house that was about to collapse, so I called out to him to get out of the way, which he did.

When the earthquake occurred. the only part of the house that collapsed was the one that had done so in my dream; the rest of the house remained standing, and nothing happened to the child, because when the earthquake happened he began running from one corner to the other in panic, moving out of the way of danger just when that particular part of the house began to collapse!

Would be it at all logical to accept as an explanation for the countless dreams of this type which accurately foretell the future the interpretations of materialists who regard all dreams as the result of the appearance in the mind of everyday events or of the fear of the unknown? Can such dreams be regarded, as the Freudians claim, simply as the reflection of repressed desires that come to the surface of the unconscious in order to delude the ego?

How can our perceptive apparatus perceive events that lie beyond the material circumstances surrounding us? How can it become aware of an event that has not yet occurred? Is there any way of explaining such awareness except in terms of a link between the human spirit and the supramaterial world?

It must then be the case that man gains awareness from the world of the unseen, from a source which is aware of the future, in just the same way that astronomical facilities permit him to record the rays emitted by the galaxies. Why should it not be accepted that the waves emitted by the world of the unseen may be picked up by the spirit of man, acting as a receiver, with the result that matters that are not knowable by natural means are made manifest in the world of dreams?

Let us take another look at what the leaders leading materialist thinkers say on the general subject of dreams:

"Contrary to what was imagined for centuries, dreams do not foretell the future or disclose any mysteries to us. The question of interpretation does not therefore arise. On the contrary, if we fully believe what Freud says, we must agree that dreams depict events out of the past. In other words, dreams result from past occurrences, and are not indications of future occurrences.

"Apart from this, careful experiments have shown that dreams — like all other 'spiritual' phenomena — are an entirely material phenomenon, without any involvement of supernatural forces."[32]

Is this really the case? Do dreams never inform us of future events or other unknown matters?

The materialists are of course free if they wish to ignore realities and to give a totally unrealistic interpretation of dreams that have nothing to do with the thoughts and occurrences of everyday life.

They pretend that their theories represent the pinnacle of perfection and they imagine they have discovered all the mysteries of the universe and the principles that govern the life of man. They suppose that whatever appears to be a mystery or resists explanation in terms of logic quite simply does not exist, so there is nothing left to explain or discover!

They should recognise, however, that such an attitude to clear and the self-evident truths is the sign of a spirit in revolt against established truths.

It is always the habit of the materialists, in their attempts to destroy the beliefs of others, to analyse hastily and impatiently whatever does not fit into their narrow framework of thought, imagining themselves able to supply answers to the most complex of questions.

However, if one studies matters soberly and patiently and attains some degree of acquaintance with non-sensory phenomena, one's vision expands and one becomes less inclined to accept monodimensional explanations.

It must not be forgotten that theologians have never denied the influence exerted on dreams by past thoughts and perceptions or by wishes and desires, as well as other factors, internal or external. Certain diseases and mental disorders cast their shadow on many dreams. But the phenomenon of the dream cannot be regarded simply as the reflection of the activity of the brain and the nervous system, or of repressed desires. Many dreams may indeed be related to such factors, but this is not the case with dreams that foretell future events. As we have seen above, such dreams cannot possibly be explained by referring to material factors and causes; they represent the distillation of a different form of reality.

* * * * *

The astounding feats of ascetics must also not be dismissed out of hand. Many people have themselves witnessed their remarkable deeds, apart from which manifest examples of their feats are recorded in numerous books of history.

If we regard the spirit as an epiphenomenon of matter, feats such as these which draw on forces hidden within man are bound to remain inexplicable.

All the various phenomena we have discussed in the past two chapters point to the existence of a reality in man that is independent of his physical being, that survives death of the body. This is the only conclusion that profound thought will yield.

If we compare man to an aeroplane made up of different components, each of which has its own function, we must agree that this aeroplane needs a skilled pilot to guide and direct it with his expertise. The pilot does not belong to the same category as the components and instruments that make up the aeroplane, although his existence is absolutely necessary for its functioning. The spirit is the pilot of the material body.

Lesson Twelve
The Ineluctable Final Moment of All Things

There can be no doubt that one day the world as it now exists
will become the scene of a terrifying event. The world which
has been the setting for man's unceasing efforts and triumphs
throughout his existence, his endeavors that have extended
from the depths of the oceans to outer space – this world will
fall prey to a horrifying fate and dissolve in a single
catastrophe.

The heavenly bodies will collide and collapse; neither
light nor warmth be left in the heavens; lofty mountains will be
uprooted; a fire will erupt as if a spark were to have fallen on a
heap of cotton that has been built up over centuries; oceans
will surge up and burst over the land; tombs will split open
and merge with each other; and the earth itself, in obedience to
divine command, will reveal and surrender all of its contents
and the trusts that have been deposited in the course of many
epochs. The whole world will be turned into a great cloud of
dust, as if everything that existed were being ground in some
gigantic mortar.

This simultaneous mingling and dispersion of all
elements, in such a way that no phenomenon can any longer be
distinguished, is the future destiny of our regular and
well-ordered world.

The Noble Qur'ān reminds man that the existing order of
creation is of limited duration and that it will not last for ever:

"*Have you not ever considered that God has created the heavens*

and the earth and all that lies between them in justice and for a set
duration? Many are those who do not believe they will meet their
Lord" (30:8).

The Qur'ān also proclaims that the occurrence of this
event is inevitable and that on the day when all creatures will
be stripped of the garment of life only the Pure and Sacred
Essence of the Creator will remain.

Let us hear the description the Qur'ān itself gives of that
terrifying day on which all things shall perish:

"*O men, fear the wrath of your Creator! The earthquakes and
explosions of resurrection will be mighty and awesome. On that day
suckling mothers will forget their infants and pregnant women will be
delivered of their burden. You will see men as drunken from the terror
of that day, but they will not be drunken, for the doom of God is fierce
and painful*" (22:1-2).

"*When the earth begins to move and shake violently, the
mountains are torn asunder and scattered like atoms of dust...*"
(56:4-6).

"*Man asks: 'When the day of resurrection will be?' (Say:) 'It well
be the day when the sight of man is confounded in terror, when the
moon is darkened and the sun and the moon are joined. On that day
man will ask where he might flee and to what shelter*" (75:6-10).

"*When the stars are put out, and when the heavenly bodies are
scattered*" (82:2).

* * * * *

Flammarion, the well-known astronomer, says in his book
The End of the World:

"The appearance of life in all its splendor is the result of
the submission of the solar system to the universal pull of
gravity and centrifugal motion. It is gravity that interrelates all
the parts of the universe, from the atom to the star, and
controls and regulates their movements with the aid of
centrifugal motion. Thus a universal order comes into being
throughout creation. This order will, however, inevitably
collapse; the stars will die and the heavenly bodies will scatter
like the beads of a broken necklace."

As can be deduced from verses of the Qur'ān and reliable narrations, the order of creation will suddenly collapse as the result of a happening the exact nature of which is unknown to us: the life of the sun, the stars and the whole of creation will come to an abrupt end.

Rill, (?) the British astronomer, says:

"The universe came into being some ten or fifteen billion years ago as the result of an explosion. It used half of its energy or its matter to dispatch the stars to the depths of space, and the other half to assemble the galaxies and prepare them for the final explosion."

The Qur'ān says: "*On the day when We shall roll up the heavens like a scroll...*" (21:104).

"*When the oceans shall be aflame...*" (81:6)

"*On the day that the heavens shall be molten like brass...*" (70:8).

The last two of these verses contradict the theory of many scientists of the past who maintained that the end of the world would come about as the result of a decrease in the heat of the sun and the freezing of all creatures. They tell instead of heat of the sun being intensified at the time of resurrection, in such a way that no living thing will be able to endure.

Many prominent scientists now describe the coming of such a day in accordance with the relative knowledge they possess.

Thus Georges Gamoff writes:

"The radiation of the sun will increase over time, and once the amount of hydrogen in the sun has attained its maximum amount, the energy emitted by the sun will increase about a hundredfold. Our studies of the production of energy by the sun thus point to conclusions that contradict completely classical quasi-official theories on the subject.

"Instead of saying that everything will freeze one day as a result of a decrease in the activity of the sun, we must say that it will be as a result of the continuing intensity of the sun's heat, during the last stage of its development, that life is condemned to destruction.

"If the temperature on the earth's surface comes to exceed

the temperature at which water boils, rocks and the hard crust of the earth will probably not melt, but the oceans will certainly begin to boil, and since no highly evolved species can live in boiling water. most forms of life will come to an end. It is therefore probable that all the higher species will have died out before the temperature of the earth reaches an intolerable level."[33]

Elsewhere the same writer remarks:

It is expected that in the course of several hundred million years after the formation of the earth's crust, the volume of the sun will come to exceed that of Venus. Its light will be multiplied ten to thirty million times, and the oceans will be brought to boiling point."[34]

The Two Trumpet Blasts of Resurrection

The Noble Qur'ān describes the occurrence of resurrection as follows:

"They will blow on the trumpet and everything in the heavens and the earth will be swallowed up by death, save only that which God wishes to preserve. Then another trumpet blast will be sounded and all creatures will suddenly rise up to behold the plain of resurrection" (39:68).

* * * * *

There will be then two blasts on the trumpet. The first will be swift and of brief duration, like a roar in the heavens, a universal proclamation that will cause the whole expanse of creation to be folded up; the people of the world will suddenly fall to the ground while they are still engrossed in their daily struggles. This first blowing of the trumpet will bring about the death of all living beings, and all creatures in the heavens and on the earth, including even the angels.

The Qur'ān says: *"On the day when the summoner (Isrāfīl) summons mankind to awesome resurrection the unbelievers will come forth with their eyes humbled, like locusts scattered abroad, hastening to respond to the summoner to resurrection. The unbelievers shall say to each other: 'This is the day of hardship!'"* (54:6-8).

The second blast on the trumpet will be the awe-inspiring summons that brings men back to life and ushers in resurrection. Men will suddenly rise up from their graves and they will ask, their whole beings filled with fear:
"Who is it that thus raises us from our slumber?" (36:52).

Then they will open their eyes and say: *"This is none other than what God promised; the prophets indeed spoke the truth"* (36:52).

Every now and then explosions take place in the heavenly bodies. Occurring in remote galaxies and the outer regions of space, these explosions do not disrupt the order of the universe or the norms of creation; their causes and effects remain, however, unknown.

It is a terrifying universal explosion that will cause the structure of the heavens and the earth to collapse, putting an end to the life of the world and its inhabitants together with the norms that have regulated creation.

The powerful waves of sound, the death-bringing blast that is a means for the implementation of the divine command, will be so intense and overwhelming that in the shortest time conceivable it will bring to an end the existence of all living things. This collapse of the world through the sound waves emitted by the trumpet of Isrāfīl will take place at a time when people are going about their daily business and are unaware that such a terrifying event is about to occur.

The Most Noble Messenger, peace and blessings be upon him and his family, said:

"At that time, some people will be in their own homelands, and some will be travelling. Some will be swallowed up by death as they are about to place a morsel of food in their mouths. Some will be talking to their friends and their souls will be taken from them before they are able to complete their words. In the end death will have overtaken all human beings, but Isrāfīl will continue blowing on his trumpet until all springs and rivers, all buildings, trees, mountains, and oceans, are intermingled and buried in the heart of the earth.

"As the dead fall to the ground, some will be on their backs, and other will lie facedown. People will still have the food in their mouths the food that death gave them no chance to swallow."[35]

* * * * *

Isrāfīl's blasts on the trumpet may be compared to the sounding of a horn that announces to an army the beginning of battle; it is like a command to get ready. The second blast is like a command to move off and attack the enemy. The trumpet has then two aspects: one of universal death and one of universal revival.

In the verses that speak of this utter reversal and transformation of the natural order, we see that terror and confusion overwhelm the whole of creation. The heavens and the earth, young and old, men and animals, all created things will be bewildered; fear will sunder all natural relations, and people will think only of themselves.

This will be the general state of all people. In addition, the impious and impure will be subject to their own special terror; they will fruitlessly desire to return to the earth in order to make up for their shameful past of disobeying God and His messengers.

But it will be too late; a fearful and majestic silence will embrace all things and none will be able to disobey God. All will set out for the divine presence in obedience to the divine summons.

God therefore calls on people to awake now in order to avoid the painful fate that ineluctably awaits sinners in the hereafter:

"O man, what deceives you concerning your Lord and makes you impudently arrogant?" (82:6).

He also warns mankind as follows:

"Before resurrection occurs and you are compelled to return to your Lord, answer the summons of your Creator. For on that day you shall have no shelter to protect you from your shameful punishment or to avert from you your well-deserved chastisement" (42:47).

Lesson Thirteen
The Resurrection of Man
in Both His Dimensions

Now let us see what the nature of life will be in the hereafter. Will resurrection be exclusively corporeal, so that man is restored to life in the material form that characterises his body, or will his eternal life be exclusively in the realm of the spirit, without any kind of attachment to the material body? Or will his return to life have on the contrary both dimensions, spiritual and semi-corporeal? Our use of the word "semicorporeal" implies that what comes to life is a subtle body, one that may be regarded as the essence of his present form. Finally, since the nature of man is a compound of body and spirit, will man's life after resurrection embrace both these dimensions, so that neither will his body — that element which gives rise to a whole series of physical and chemical reaction — perish completely, nor will his spirit be the separated from his bodily form?

All these represent various theories put forward concerning the nature of resurrection; let us now examine each one in turn.

Some scholars espouse the first theory and say that when death overtakes the body and its physical and chemical reactions are brought to an end, everything reaches its point of termination. However, when resurrection takes place, the scattered form of man is reassembled out of the particles that have been buried in the earth, scattered in the air, or drowned in the ocean. When the body thus begins its new life, the spirit — which counts as one of the properties of the mechanism of the body — is bound also to come back to life.

The second theory has also been espoused by many philosophers. They believe that since the spirit represents both the source and the essence of human existence and its very structure predisposes it to continual life, it bids eternal farewell to the material body when death occurs for the structure of the body predisposes it to perishing. After enjoying for a brief time the life-giving rays of the spirit, the body finds that its role is at an end. The compound nature of the body permitted it to house the abstract spirit only for a limited time, after which it inevitably fell prey to decay and death. The spirit, by contrast, being ultimately free of the body and its properties, remains eternal and immortal, and it is therefore the spirit alone which appears on the plain of resurrection. Were this not the case, resurrection would have no meaning. This theory implies, of course, that punishment and reward are exclusively moral or spiritual.

There is no firm evidence in support of this theory, but it used to have many supporters. Now it has very few followers, for the realistic theories put forward by scholars have thoroughly undermined it.

The third analysis of the question is that which was made by a number of ancient philosophers. They said that when we die, our body is indeed destroyed: its elemental and material elements are dissolved in such a way that they cannot be reassembled. The spirit then remains, but not in a state of utter abstraction; it is lodged in a subtle body that is not capable of physical and chemical reactions but nonetheless resembles our present body. This subtle body, also known as the imaginal body, is extraordinarily active and has the ability to transcend all obstacles, and is able to live eternally.

There is yet a fourth theory, which is held by many theologians and philosophers both of the past and the present. It is based on the principle that resurrection represents a complete and comprehensive return to life for nothing that pertains to man can ever be fully destroyed. Man resumes his life in the next world with all his qualities and properties, the only difference being that his resurrectional life unfold in a more elevated realm than this world. On that plane we will attain a state in which matter and spirit retain their separate essences but become so closely interrelated that their existence becomes manifest as a single unit.

The reality of resurrectional life must be envisaged, according to the view, as containing both dimensions of man, not separate but joined, just as was the case in this world.

* * * * *

No intellectual argument can be advanced as evidence for the nature of life after death; it is only the necessity of resurrection and its simultaneously spiritual and physical nature that are topics for philosophical and rational analysis. Philosophy and the intellect have no key for unlocking the mystery of which, out of all possible forms, will definitely occur in the hereafter. Nonetheless, when we look at the way in which the last of the theories outlined above seeks to answer this question, we see that it contains an element of truth, for it points in the same direction as the authoritative texts of Islam and is compatible with them.

The Qur'ān — which is the principal source for all such topics — repeatedly states that resurrection will be bodily. It proclaims, clearly and unmistakably, that man will be resurrected with the body he has had in this world. The verses in question are indeed so explicit as to leave no room for symbolic interpretation. Consider, for example, these verses:

"God begins creation, then He renews it, and after that causes it to return to Him" (30:11).

"Does man imagine that We will not gather together his bones? We are able to recreate even the tips of his fingers" (75:3-4).

The second of these two verses states that those who imagine the body to be incapable of renewed life, after the dissolution and scattering of its particles, are, in reality, unaware of God's infinite power; they do not understand that the reconstruction of human life out of the scattered particles of the body, even to the extent of reproducing the minutiae of the fingertips, represents a small and insignificant task for the boundless power of the Creator.

"*Say: 'He will give life to the bones Who created them for the first time; certainly He is aware of all His creation*'" (36:79).

A Story from the Qur'ān

The Noble Qur'ān presents narratives concerning the prophets 'Uzayr and Ibrāhīm, the Friend of God, each of which includes a living example of bodily resurrection. God clarifies the matter for each of these great prophets by placing before them a concrete example of dead forms being restored to life once the necessary circumstances come to obtain by divine order: the spirit becomes manifest anew in the body so that its life resumes.

We read in the story of 'Uzayr that mounted on his donkey he once came across a ruin in the course of a journey. In that ruin he was confronted by the dreadful sight of the rotting bones of men who had long since died. He plunged deep into thought and asked himself, "How will God bring these back to life?"

At that very moment God took his soul, but one hundred years later He brought him back to life. He asked him, "How long have you been here?" He immediately answered, "One day or less."

'Uzayr was then informed that he had been in that place for a hundred years, lying lifeless on the ground exactly where he had fallen. He was instructed to look at his donkey, and saw that its body was thoroughly decomposed: then God brought it back life.

In the story of 'Uzayr, we also see that in order to demonstrate the limitlessness of His power God preserved water and foodstuffs intact for a hundred years, objects that decay or vaporise more quickly than living beings on account of their exposure to natural factors such as heat, sunlight, wind and dust. He addressed 'Uzayr as follows:

"Look at your food and drink; it has not changed and it shows no sign of age. Look too at your donkey, so that its story becomes apparent to you and We may make of you a proof for people so that they no longer deny resurrection. Look at the rotten bones, and see how We bring them together and make flesh grow on them. When all this was shown clearly to him (the verse continues), *he said, 'I know now for certain that God is empowered over all things'"* (2:259).

The Qur'ān depicts another concrete instance of bodily resurrection in one of the narratives concerning Ibrāhīm, upon whom be peace. It tells with the utmost clarity how Ibrāhīm witnessed with his own eyes the reassembling of the scattered particles of a body:

"When Ibrāhīm said: 'O God, show me how you bring the dead back to life,' God responded, 'Do you not believe?' He said, 'I do, but I wish my heart to be reassured.' So God said, 'Choose four types of birds, and mix their flesh together, and place portions on the top of mountains. Then summon the birds, and they will come hastening to you. You will then know that God is empowered over all things and is aware of the truth of all things'" (2:260).

Ibrāhīm was rationally and logically convinced of the truth of resurrection, but he wished also to witness it in sensory fashion. He posed the very wise question of how the dead are brought back to life.

One may believe in a variety of things without being aware of their precise nature, a simple example being that we believe in the reality of radio and television without knowing anything of how the sounds and images reach us.

Ibrāhīm believed in the principle of resurrection and the renewal of life, but he wished also to understand how the dead are brought back to life, to know it directly by means of a concrete example, and to satisfy his inner feelings by means of sensory experience.

After Ibrāhīm witnessed that remarkable scene, he was instructed to ponder upon it and to realize that God is capable of all things and that given His infinite knowledge and power it is a small matter for Him to identify and reassemble the scattered particles of the dead.

Imām al-Sajjād, upon whom be peace, said:

"At the time of resurrection men's bodies will grow out of the ground like plants. The particles that were transformed into earth will rejoin each other, through the will and the power of God, so that if even a thousand people should have been buried in the same grave and their flesh and their rotting bones intermingled, they will separate on the day of resurrection; the earthly remains of each dead person will be quite distinct."[36]

There are many clear verses in the Qur'ān, additional to those we have cited, which point clearly to the nature of resurrection. They refute all restriction of renewed life to the spirit, using such expressions such as "*God will certainly resurrect the dead from their tombs*" (22:6).

In another verse we read, "*You will return to Him just as He created you*" (7:29).

In concise and eloquent fashion, this verse draws the attention of man to his original creation, reminding him how the form of his body was fashioned from the various solid elements of the earth and from water. The different elements which were compounded in him had first existed in the form of foodstuffs — fruits and vegetables scattered over the face of the earth or drops of water taken from the depths of the ocean to be transformed into vapor and rain. Why then should man not believe that those same materials, separated from each other and scattered by wind and by storm, will be gathered together again and resume their previous shape and form? If the restoration of life is impossible, how is it that an exactly similar process took place at the beginning of creation?

From the moment that the spirit is connected to the human body, a special kind of union between the two comes into existence which becomes deeper and more complete with the passage of time. A precise and subtle affinity and harmony comes to prevail, as a result of which spirit and body fall under each other's influence; attributes of the spirit appear in the body, and attributes of the body appear in the spirit. Even the occurrence of death and the separation of the spirit from the body combined with its transfer to another world do not bring this affinity to an end. The various changes that the spirit and the particles of the body separately undergo also fail to affect this affinity, and although the earthly particles of the body exist in different material circumstances from before, they retain their links with the spirit.

Thus the material body and the non-material spirit are linked through the very circumstances of their origin; acquiring a whole series of shared characteristics that further join them together, they retain their affinity throughout the changes and motions they separately undergo.

A corollary of this is that hidden within every drop of sperm are both spiritual characteristics and physical properties.

The affinity between body and spirit causes each spirit to incline in the direction of the body and its particles, by means of the appropriate motions that have come to adhere to the spirit, and also attracts each body towards the spirit, in accordance with a particular set of circumstances and a series of divinely decreed norms. After passing through various stages of change the body leaves its earthly form behind and by an act of God is transformed into a more perfect form, in which it resumes its close link and union with the spirit.

It is worth mentioning that the changes mentioned above are also repeated in the world of being. The earthly particles of our present body are the result of transformations that have taken place because of a specific set of causes. Not only does the body take shape by means of those transformations; each body also is constantly renewed through the decay of the elements and particles that compose it and the replacement of those elements and particles by new ones.

The Noble Qur'ān says the following about the comprehensive and all-embracing transformation by means of which the whole order of being will be changed into something other than itself:

"*The day on which the heavens and earth will be changed into other than the heavens and earth, and all will be brought before God, the One and All-Powerful*" (14:48).

The earthly particles of the human body follow therefore

the general transformations that the whole order of being undergoes; they are transformed, in fact, in conjunction with the totality of that order, taking on a more complete aspect in which their true nature becomes apparent and man recovers his true being.

It must be remarked that although the body man will possess in the hereafter is fashioned from the particles of his present body and has the same shape, it will nonetheless have acquired new characteristics which are incompatible with the recognized criteria of this world and are inconceivable to our minds. Our body in the hereafter will be capable of new effects fully compatible with that realm, the comprehension of which, together its interrelations and the norms that govern it, requires a higher consciousness than we now possess.

* * * * *

The Qur'ān says the following, in expounding another matter concerning bodily resurrection;

"*When they enter hellfire, their eyes and ears and the skins on their bodies shall give witness against them on account of the sins they have committed. They will address their skins asking them, 'Why do you give witness against us?' They will receive this answer: 'The Lord Who gave speech to all things and Who first created you has given speech to us, too; certainly you will return to him,*" (41:20-21).

Here a remarkable, indeed shattering scene is described. No one expects the organs of his own body to rise up and bear witness against him in the tribunal of the hereafter. The skin of the body, which is closer to man than any other part of his physical being, has been chosen to testify concerning him. Those who used to sin and do wrong in secret, because of their defective notions about the reach of God's knowledge, who strove to conceal the ugliness of their acts from the view of others, will see on that day that their eyes and the skin of their bodies, transformed into an organ of vision, have stood up to give testimony against them. In their astonishment they will therefore ask the organs of their bodies: "Why are you giving testimony against us?" They will receive a firm answer, delivered in tones of reproach by their bodily organs, "He is the Creator Who first brought you into existence and to Him you will return."

* * * * *

The Commander of the Faithful, 'Alī, upon whom be peace, said:

"Matters will succeed each other and ages will pass away, one after the other, until resurrection finally arrives. Then God will bring men forth from the pits of their tombs, from the nests of ravenous birds, from the lairs of wild animals, and from battlefields. They will hasten toward the divine presence, in obedience to God's command, to be sent on to their eternal abode. They will stand before Him, silent and in groups. Although their numbers will be vast, none of them will be hidden from God's limitless knowledge and penetrating vision."[37]

Certain verses also mention the body that man will have at resurrection as being similar to his body in this world. An example is: "*Although the skin on their body will burn, We will clothe them in new skins so they may taste the severity of our torment*" (4:56).

A terrifying panorama of prolonged sensory torment is conjured up here, showing that the painful punishment of the sinners will be constantly repeated.

Verses such as this in no way contradict the verses previously quoted, because the constantly renewed skins are fashioned from the same original skin; it is there alone that change and increase or decrease may take place.

It will be fitting an explanation given by Imām al-Ṣādiq, on whom be peace, which clarifies the lack of contradiction involved.

Someone once asked Imām al-Ṣādiq what sin those various skins had committed to make them deserving of chastisement. He answered that from one point of view they are the same as the original skin and from another point of view different from them. The man then asked him to explain the matter further by means of a comparison. The Imām said: "Have you ever seen someone break a brick, and then pour it in a mold and restore it to its original shape? From one point of view the second brick is identical with the first, and from another point of view it is different from it."[38]

Once the Prophet of Islam was speaking about bodily resurrection, a subject that was baffling, inexplicable and even unacceptable for the polytheists. They reacted therefore with their customary stupidity.

In that milieu where obsolete criteria and destructive superstitions had taken the place of free thought and decay had spread like the plague destroying the fabric of society, it was the aim of the Qur'ān to guide the ailing minds of men to a search for the truth. The Qur'ān thus reproduces the words of those foolish ones as follows:

"The unbelievers shall say: 'Shall we show to you a man who says that after you die and the particles of your body are scattered, you will be brought back to life? Is such a person a liar against God or is it lunacy that impels him to utter such words?' No, it is those who do not believe in resurrection who will suffer torment in the hereafter and here they are misguided, far distant from salvation" (34:7-8).

All these clear and categorical verses, which leave no room for symbolic interpretation, speak unmistakably of bodily resurrection.

To approach the matter from a different point of view, certain deductions can be made that permit us to conclude that the body and the soul are two entities linked together the mutual inclination of which brings man into being: whatever motion or activity arises from man in this world bear within it a part of both elements.

If we view the matter in this way, not only is there no need to postulate a separation between body and soul; we are also provided with a realistic indication that the two must necessarily be compounded anew in life after death.

We know that neither body nor soul represents a complete entity in itself if isolated from the other. The body is an instrument of the soul, and the role it plays in assuring the continuous activity of the soul is crucial.

All legislators throughout history have regarded legal and penal provisions as being addressed to man in both the dimensions of which he is compounded, the bodily and the spiritual, so that neither of these dimensions is forced to bear the burden of responsibility alone. In similar fashion, both dimensions are called to account jointly for their deeds when the final reckoning is made on the plain of resurrection.

Is it, indeed, conceivable that man should be held as legally accountable in this world with both dimensions, but in the hereafter all responsibility should be placed on the fragile shoulders of his spirit?

The fundamental purpose of resurrection is that human beings should attain ultimate felicity and complete the final stages of their development, by virtue of the pure belief they have held and the good deeds they have performed. The attainment of such an aim requires careful and precise planning, and all divine religions have therefore laid down a series of precepts and commands the fulfilment of which will enable man to reach the lofty summit for which he is destined.

The most practical and effective method for the fulfilment of this plan consists of simultaneously encouraging man and inducing fear in him; on the one hand establishing reward and giving the glad tidings of the infinite blessings of paradise, and on the other hand threatening him with punishment and warning him of torment and unendurable pain. Both reward and punishment must be recognizable and perceptible to ordinary human perception for the final outcome of good deeds and the abandonment of evil to become firmly rooted in man's inner being.

Purely spiritual rewards and punishments would not be comprehensible for the masses of humanity; it is corporeal enjoyment and torment that are capable of arousing their attention. They both encourage man to do good deeds, in obedience to the law, and inspire in him fear of the consequences of violating the law.

For most people, the concept of pleasure is simultaneously

corporeal and spiritual; few indeed are those who could adequately grasp the notion of purely spiritual pleasure or punishment.

This being the case, to promise men infinite joys of a spiritual nature or to warn them of an exclusively spiritual torment would not work a transforming effect in the depths of men's soul; it would be unable to control the disparate tendencies at work within man or to prevent him from entering the forbidden zone of sin.

It is only those whom God has chosen as His friends and possess accordingly sublime minds in whose souls the anticipation of non-material rewards will arouse the desire to obey – even to love – God's commands.

In addition, God's abundant favor and wisdom necessitate that He bestows all conceivable material and non-material blessings on His pure, sincere, and devoted servants, and that He should punish bloodthirsty and bestial tyrants with a comprehensive punishment that is both material and non-material. The comprehensiveness both of blessedness in the hereafter and of requital can be assured only by man being resurrected in both his dimensions.

The Qur'ān promises both material and spiritual blessings to the virtuous and the pious:

"*God promises the believers, both women and men, that He will cause them to enter a paradise where rivers flow beneath the trees, and have them dwell in splendid palaces. He will also bestow on them His pleasure and satisfaction, which is greater and loftier than material bounties. This spiritual reward is, in truth, the supreme achievement for the pure*" (9:72).

* * * * *

The Limited Capacity of the Earth

Some people might voice the objection that the globe cannot possibly accommodate on the day of resurrection all the human beings who have lived upon it throughout time. This objection is, however, completely unfounded, because as the Qur'ān makes entirely clear, the orderly rotation of the heavens will be thoroughly disrupted when the end of the world comes. An awesome power will grind the mountains into dust and scatter them in every direction; the sun and the moon will lose their familiar splendor and light and grow dark; and the whole coherent order of the universe, formed of sublime phenomena that are fashioned from the crudest of materials, will utterly collapse. An entirely new order and structure of creation will come into being on the silent and dead ruins of the old.

It can, then, be easily understood that any objection based on an alleged lack of space on the globe is quite unwarranted.

Those whose system of thought is opposed to the view of believers in God and who are accustomed to raising all kinds of objections also raise another question. They point out that the cells in the human body are replaced annually so that every individual changes his physical form several times in the course of his life, gradually and imperceptibly. Now it is obvious that every body performs acts, in the course of its specific lifespan, that deserve reward or punishment; which body will it be, however, that must ultimately held responsible for those deeds at the time of resurrection?

The answer to this objection in obvious. Given the fact that each new cell inherits the characteristics and attributes of its predecessor so that even the external appearance of the body is indistinguishable from the old, it is plain that the final body of man represents a compendium of the attributes of all the preceding bodies.

The resurrection of the last body which is visible to us is therefore tantamount to the resurrection of all its predecessors.

Scarcity of Matter and the Multitude of Men

Another objection which is raised is that of the limited nature of the earthly materials which contain in themselves the remains of countless men who have been turned into earth. It is said that the amount of earth presently available will not suffice for the fashioning anew of so many people.

The baselessness of this objection, which does not

originate in any serious search for the truth, becomes obvious when we make the following calculations.

Every square kilometer of earth is enough for making a hundred million men. This amount occupies a very paltry portion of the earth's surface, but it would be enough for refashioning twenty times the present population of the world.

Based on this calculation, an extremely small plot of land would yield enough material for making anew the bodies of billions upon billions of men, so the objection that the raw materials needed for resurrecting so many people would be lacking turns out to be groundless.

Furthermore, one of the properties of matter is that it takes on different forms. If for example the atoms comprising one cubic meter of stone are split, they can occupy millions of cubic meters of space; their dimensions expand to an unimaginable degree.

The Qur'ān proclaims: "*A day will come on which the earth will be transformed into other than itself*" (14:48).

The Eater and the Eaten

There is a very ancient and interesting objection that we should not pass over in silence. This relates to the transformation of the particles of the bodies of the deceased into substances that are then consumed by others, causing those particles to become intermingled with the bodies of others.

It is true that not a single human body can be found which is entirely free of contamination by other elements. However, this intermingling with alien substances is so slight, in the circumstances of this world, both quantitatively and qualitatively, as to be imperceptible. However, it is conceivable that when bodies are reconstructed in the hereafter a kind of rivalry and struggle for the possession of certain materials may take place.

It is entirely possible that this struggle should not be confined to two individuals, taking place instead among a number of claimants each seeking possession of a certain particle as its true owner. Who should in fact take possession of it?

This then is the problem.

When we look back to the first sign of life, we see that we began as monocellular beings. Then our body took shape through the multiplication and growth of the different parts and limbs of our body. In the past, it was imagined that our personality and our physical charactertistics were contained only in the mass of reproductive cells, but it is known now that they are present within each individual cell. Each cell acts separately as a mirror in which the whole appearance of man is reflected. This holds true not only of man but also of all other living creatures.

This being the case, if even a single cell from man's body, with the entirety of his personality inscribed within it, is placed in suitable circumstances, it is capable of undertaking by itself the entire task of reconstructing the body, through dividing and giving birth to new cells.

Now if particles of the body become absorbed into the structure of another, the particles belonging to that individual will return to their original locus. By thus returning the particles it had borrowed from a stranger, the second body will in fact be preserving its own original being. It should also be stressed that since each of the two bodies retains its respective characteristics even though their constituent elements become intermingled, there is nothing to prevent each of them from displaying anew its respective identity. Even if the original particles left over from each body be exceedingly few — even if, for example, only a single cell survives — it will still be possible for that body to reconstruct itself, and nothing can prevent it from doing so.

In any event, irrespective of whether the work of repair and reconstruction be completed swiftly or gradually, every particle retains the capacity of building anew the original body, just as that body once emerged from a single drop of sperm.

The same problem can be solved in another way.

As we know, the body is engaged in constant dissolution

and replacement. The entire bodily frame changes once every few years, gradually and imperceptibly. If a person appropriates elements of the being of another, directly or indirectly, using them to nurture himself, it is obvious that only a part of that stranger becomes intermingled with him, for he is, after all, a complete person in his own right. Out of all the nutrition that a person consumes, only three percent is absorbed into his body. Why then should the remaining ninety seven percent which is not absorbed into the body, not be available for the resurrection of the individual with whom they originated?

Apart from this, in accordance with the laws of physics, all forms of energy in the world may be transformed into each other, given the appropriate conditions. Man is himself a source for the production of energy and even after his death his body is transformed from one form of energy into another. At the time of resurrection, all the energies of living beings will exist in utter freedom, and they will be able to return to their original form by means of a kind of inverted reaction. The mere fact that we do not know precisely how this change will take place does not give us the right to dismiss it as impossible.

As for punishment in the hereafter, it should be realized that what causes pain and torment has a connection to the spirit, so that if part of the body of a believer become attached to that of an unbeliever, it is the unbeliever that will suffer the pain of torment not the believer.

In addition to all the foregoing, it must be stated that it is entirely possible for God to restore life to a body that has changed, gradually and imperceptibly, the cells composing its brain, nerves and bones, as much as ten times in the course of a lifetime. Any individual today is different from what he was ten years ago. It is a matter of indifference to which of those versions of the body the spirit be rejoined at resurrection, for that upon which the humanity of an individual depends and which serves as the guarantor of the uniqueness of his personality, is the non-material spirit, which is charged with the administration and governance of his body from its first appearance until death.

From the first beginning of creation down to the present, billions of human beings have come into existence, and even if they now lie intermingled with each other, the spiritual characteristics of each of them remain utterly distinct. If a person committed a crime ten years ago, it cannot be said that since his physical form has changed, he should not be tried in place of that person who committed the crime ten years ago.

If we offset a book, the new printing will be exactly the same as the old, although the paper and binding may be different.

Since man needs matter as the means whereby he manifests his existence, he must necessarily be resurrected with his body. However, it is not at all necessary that an individual come back to life at resurrection with all the forms his body has had from birth to death; it can be said that they all appear together in a single form at the time of resurrection.

If this be true, it completely disposes of the objection that particles which have transferred from one body to another cannot be simultaneously present in two persons at the time of resurrection.

Furthermore, the real dimensions of the body are composed of a single insignificant atom; the rest is made up of empty space. If some powerful form of pressure were brought to bear on the body, making it compact and eliminating the spaces between its electrons, the basic matter of the body would be seen to be a minute atom visible only to a microscope.

It is therefore not at all necessary for the spaces between the particles of the body to be recreated at resurrection; it will be quite sufficient for the particles themselves (either some of them or all of them) to return.

None of the possibilities mentioned above should be regarded as categorical answers to the problems posed by the restoration of life to man; they are merely avenues to understanding that lie within our reach. We cannot restrict our reflections on this subject to the arguments set out above. Our aim has been only to prove that doubts and objections such as

those we have reviewed should not be allowed to affect our
basic belief in resurrection and the restoration of life to the
body which is so strongly emphasized by the revealed
religions, especially the Qur'ān.

Lesson Fourteen
Characteristics of the Hereafter

The images that we form in our minds of persons, gardens, cities or other places when we hear them described to us, are generally quite different from we later see when we come to observe the objects at first hand. This is true despite the fact that we have often seen similar objects earlier in our lives and are therefore able to make comparisons.

When we wish to give some idea of the bliss or punishment that awaits man in the hereafter, the vocabulary we have at our disposal in this world is clearly inadequate to delineate an accurate picture. The reality will not in an way conform to our mental deductions.

It is not easy for us to perceive the painful torments that sinners will justly endure and the countless blessings that await the believer, for we have never beheld or touched them. They belong to the realm of the unseen; we are unable to experience them directly, and our mind is not equipped to comprehend their precise and true sense. The images we have of concretely existing objects cannot be extended to cover a reality that lies beyond our reach and experience.

The terms and expressions that we have in our vocabulary are designed for the limited affairs and concerns of this world. This is all we have at our disposal — words the reach of which not extend beyond the four walls of our present world.

A different vocabulary and a different mode of vision are therefore required for perceiving and understanding matters that lie beyond this limited realm.

Although the life of this world and that of the hereafter have certain aspects in common, both representing forms of life in which pleasure and pain, joy and sorrow, are present, there are also profound and fundamental differences between them.

In this world, life begins with infancy and ends with old age, but no such change or transformation exists in the hereafter. Here man must labor and sow; there he reaps.

Thus the Commander of the Faithful said:

"Today is the day of work, not the day of accounting; tomorrow is the day of accounting, not the day of work."[39]

In this world the rays of man's awareness can illuminate for him a realm that appears extensive to him but is in reality finite, whereas in the hereafter human perception attains its utmost expansion and become unlimited.

Defects, lacks and sicknesses constantly plague man in this world, but the very concept of these is non-existent in the hereafter. There, perfection, happiness and purity exist in the most sublime form. In this world, man is constantly striving to gain possession of what he does not have, and he is never satisfied with what he acquires. In the hereafter, he never experiences the tormenting feeling of lack, for God wills that whatever he desires should immediately be placed at his disposition. Apart from this, he will have attained there the true object of his love; he will be in the presence of the One in painful separation from Whom he has grieving and lamenting. There is therefore absolutely nothing left for him to desire, and none among the dwellers in paradise could wish for any change in his state.

The Qur'ān says the following concerning the unique characteristics of the blessings of paradise and the unique happiness they bestow, not in any way comparable to the enjoyments of this world:

"*The likeness of the paradise that has been promised to the Godfearing is a garden where flow beneath trees; its foods will be constantly available, and the shade there will be permanent*" (13:35).

Only a pale and inevitably deficient portrayal of the

blessings of paradise can be given for the inhabitants of this finite world. The verse therefore offers an approximate and allusive description of paradise; what will ultimately present itself to us as paradise is infinitely more sublime than the gardens of this world and the joys of walking freely among trees in the fresh morning air.

The fruits of the hereafter are not tied to any season or subject to blight; they are constantly within reach of the blessed. The shade cast by the trees of paradise bear no resemblance to the shade of trees in this world, which gradually shifts in accordance with the motion of the sun, or even disappears once autumn strips the trees of their leaves. In short, like all the other blessings of paradise, the shade of paradise is eternal and it holds its denizens at all times in its gentle embrace.

In the final analysis, the Qur'ān clearly recognizes the inability of man to grasp and perceive the characteristics of paradise and says:

"None can perceive what blessings are hidden for man in that realm which will delight his eye" (32:17).

Furthermore, there is no limitation, with respect to type and category, that will be placed on the blessings of paradise:

"Whatever the heart desires and delights the eye will be brought into being" (43:71).

* * * * *

We know that God's acts are implemented by means of His all-powerful will; as soon as He wills a certain thing, its existence on the plain of being follows automatically. Thus the Qur'ān says:

"Whatsoever We will to exist and command to come into being, that very instant it comes into being without any delay" (16:40).

One of the distinguishing features of the hereafter is that the dwellers in paradise will reach a point at which their deeds come to resemble the acts of God; they rely on their wills for the accomplishment of their deeds, without the need for physical strength or means and instruments.

The Qur'ān says concerning the life of the blessed in the hereafter:

"*They have whatever they wish and desire*" (39: 34).

The Commander of the Faithful, upon whom be peace, said:

"The fruits of the hereafter are plucked without any effort; desire and inclination suffice to obtain them."[40]

Security and Peace

One of the fundamental differences between life in this world and life in the hereafter is that the relationships prevailing in the latter are utterly different from those found in the material world, because of the sublime and perfect nature of the hereafter.

In this world, beings infringe on each other, because of the particular type of relationships that exist here and the conditions created by time and space. By contrast, in the hereafter none will find his own existence threatened by that of another, and none of the relations prevailing there will be based on negation or repulsion; all relationships will revolve around an axis of security and peace. The closer in the hierarchy of existence a sphere of being is situated to the Exalted Origin of all being, the greater will be the degree of unity and harmony it possesses, and the farther removed it will be from separation, contradiction, and opposition. Once man reaches the sublime realm of the hereafter and enters the proximity of God's mercy, he will be beyond the reach of the unpleasant contingencies of the material world. Conversely, the farther removed a sphere of being is in the hierarchy of existence from the Effulgent Principle of all existence and the lower its rank, the more severe will be the contradictions that prevail in it and the more widespread will be the processes of mutual rejection and denial at work in it.

The Qur'ān says the following concerning the relationships prevailing in the hereafter:

"*In truth, the Godfearing shall have gardens with flowing rivers in paradise. They will be invited to enter eternal paradise to the accompaniment of greetings and peace and in the enjoyment of utter respect and security. We will utterly purify their hearts of all darkness, hatred and envy, and all other undesirable characteristics, so that will treat each other as brothers and friends and will sit facing each other on thrones of dignity. No pain or grief shall afflict them, and they shall never be banished from paradise"* (15:45-48).

In another verse, the Qu'rān refers to the order prevailing in paradise by the them "The Abode of Peace." It is an order in which all things will exist and interrelate on a basis of peace, because entry to such a pure realm — one free of all defect and contradiction — is necessitated precisely by their uniform motion toward God and their attainment of proximity to the Origin of all being. Thus the Qur'ān says: *"They shall have abode of peace and security in the presence of their Lord; God shall be their friend and protector for they were doers of good"* (6:127).

Awesome Torment and Shattering Punishment

The human intellect and powers of perception of man are also incapable of grasping the true nature of punishment in the hereafter; there is no tongue capable of describing the torment that the Creator will inflict. The Qur'ān provides the following description of the painful state that will be the lot of the damned in hellfire:

"The fire of hell will burn them from within and will then proceed outwards; its first spark will strike the heart" (104:6-7).

How terrible is the furnace which will be fueled with the bodies of the sinners as well as the stones of hell! Let us see what the Qur'ān says about it:

"Death will confront them on every hand, there is no question of their dying, for their torment will be severe and eternal" (14:17).

The Commander of the Faithful, peace be upon him, said the following in the *Du'a-yi Kumayl* concerning God's wrathful punishment and the terrifying spectacle of eternal torment:

"However great and fearsome be the torments and trials of this world, they are like a game when compared to the torment and punishment of the hereafter. The hardships and pains of this world are slight and of limited duration, but punishment in the hereafter lasts for all eternity. No clemency or commutation will be available to those who have earned that punishment, for the punishment is a fire kindled by God's wrath, anger and vengeance. So grievous is that torment that neither the heavens nor the earth can endure it."

* * * * *

In order for eternity to come about, it would be enough for God to remove the principle of entropy from matter; the particularities and characteristics of the hereafter would then come into view, and everything — pain and pleasure, all living beings — would take on the aspect of eternity. The lash of death and destruction would no longer fall on the shoulders of all beings, and we would live eternally in the present world, the cause of corruption and death having been removed from it.

We must therefore address our Lord as follows, with utter sincerity:

"*O Creator, keep distant from us the torment of hellfire, for indeed that torment is grievous and permanent*" (25:65).

The believer who is firmly convinced that the day of requital will come, who knows that the place of the sinner and the oppressor will be the low levels and regions of hell, will fear the outcome of his deeds. However much one exercises vigilance over the self and strives to remember that God Almighty is aware of all things, it is still possible that under the influence of instinctual urge he may fall into the pit of sin and impurity. One of the ways to protect oneself against such lapses is therefore to appeal to God's infinite kindness and confess to his sins and shortcomings.

When confessing to his sins, man should in the first place address himself with the command to abandon all sin. Reminding himself that hell is an evil abode, he warns himself not to transgress the limits set by God and to reflect on the residence he wishes to occupy in the hereafter. He aspires to the abode that overflows with the blessings of God and has been made ready for the pure and Godfearing.

As soon as man's inward relationship with God begins to

weaken, and he begins to distance himself from a firm rooting in faith, the entirety of his being becomes a hunting ground for demons who rob him of all virtue, piety, and the capacity for salvation.

Conversely, steadfastness on God's path and constancy in implementing His commands protect the heart of man from satanic thoughts and inclinations. Since man is full of weaknesses and defects, he ought always take refuge in the source of all good and evil to protect himself against the danger of sin.

The Noble Qur'ān declares to men that they should take refuge with God from whatever pulls in the direction of rebellion and disobedience to divine command and thus leads them astray.

"Say: 'I seek refuge in the Lord of mankind, the Sovereign over manking, the God of mankind, from the evil of satan, the satan that inspires evil thoughts in the hearts of mankind and belongs either to the category of jinn or to that of mankind'" (114:1-6).

"Satan incites you to ugly and forbidden acts with the fear of poverty, but God promises you forgiveness and generosity; His compassion is infinite and He is All-Knowing" (2:268).

It is true that God's mercy and kindness are universal in their extent, but this should not be taken as negating the principle of punishment and requital. One cannot interpret God's compassion and generosity in a sense that requires Him to love transgression, cruelty, and injustice, or treat uniformly the oppressor and the oppressed.

His justice requires Him to give to everyone in accordance with his need and his state; it is this wise principle, this all-encompassing law of divine justice, that ensures the firm orderliness of the world.

The Noble Qur'ān says:

"O Messenger, the unbelievers ask you whether what you say concerning religion and the day of resurrection is true. Tell them, 'Yes, I swear by God that all the threats and promises are true, and you will have no escape from God's punishment.' If on that day the oppressors rule the entire face of the world and wish to sacrifice all

their wealth in the hope of saving themselves from punishment, they will be unable to do so. When they witness the torment, they will conceal their regret in order not to give joy to their adversaries. They shall be judged in justice, and no injustice will be involved in their punishment. Be aware, O mankind, that whatever exists in the heavens and on earth is God's, but most men are unaware. It is God who brings men to life, Who causes the living to die, and it is to Him that you will return" (10:53-56).

When man enters the world, in accordance with the will of a power higher than himself, he naturally stands in need of that infinite power. He is lowly and humble when confronted with that Absolute One. Were that Exalted Being, empowered as He is over all powerful and arrogant tyrants, not to punish disobedient despots by humbling them before Him, then justice and wisdom would lose all their meaning.

Should God prepare a kind reception in the hereafter for those bloodthirsty tyrants who have blackened the pages of history with their shameful deeds, or make ready for them a secure place of enjoyment? Does not the torment of hellfire represent true justice and therefore mercy for them?

Can any intelligent man push the belief in the meaninglessness and absurdity of the world to the point of imagining that bloodthirsty and evil men will be free of all punishment for their deeds? Can the slightest evidence for such a degree of meaninglessness be found anywhere in the universe?

One can see indications of the torment of the hereafter in the remorse and regret that are experienced by sinners when their conscience begins to weigh heavy upon them. This remorse is like a small hell that troubles and burns the heart of the sinner; it is an indication that a means for assessing good and evil and measuring men's deeds exists within the very order of creation.

One cannot call God just and merciful unless He punishes the corrupt for their deeds, for it is His absolute justice that prevents an atom's weight of good and an atom's weight of evil from remaining unaccounted for.

The Commander of the Faithful, upon whom be peace, said:

"If God gives respite to the oppressor, his punishment is never cancelled. Not only are his comings and goings under God's surveillance; He watches his gullet closely and what passes down it."[41]

He also said, in similar vein:

"I swear by God that if my hands and feet were to be chained, and I were made to turn back and forth, night and day, on a bed of thorns, I would prefer it to meeting God and His Messenger on the day of resurrection as one who had oppressed people and usurped their wealth."[42]

Fear of One's Deeds

The exemplars of religion have always emphasised the fear of God goes back in fact to men's fear of their own deeds. Not only is this fear not harmful; it is extremely beneficial in that it keeps man's deeds in balance and under control. Fear of the unpleasant consequences of sin induces caution in man and helps him to rein in his rebellious instincts; it makes him a disciplined and orderly being.

If man were only to place his hope in the infinite mercy of God, with an unbridled optimism not balanced with fear, the result would be the transgression of all limits. The one whose heart is filled only with the hope of God's mercy will feel absolutely free to engage in any foolish and corrupt act he wishes; he will still hope for God's mercy and regard himself as worthy of God's forgiveness despite all the abominations he has committed. Such a person will never think of obeying God nor will he aspire to purity; his entire conduct will be suffused with corruption, but he will entertain hopes of a bright future.

Since, then, the absence of fear of God leads to corruption and sinful behavior, religion prescribes that man should alternate between hope and fear: while hoping for God's infinite mercy and generosity, man should reflect carefully and soberly on the consequences of his deeds, fearing their possible outcome.

On the other hand, if we completely abandon our hope of
God's favor and kindness, our belief in a better future, in
bright horizons where we can compensate for our sins and
acquire virtue, would be threatened. All the spiritual
potentialities which might one day blossom forth as a result of
our constant exertions would remain buried for ever.

The Commander of the Faithful, upon whom be peace,
said:

"Do not consider even the purest member of this
community as safe from divine punishment, for the Qur'ān
tells us, *'It is only those who stand to lose that feel safe against God's
punishment.'* Likewise, do not cause the most evil of men to
despair of God's mercy and favor, for God says, *'Only the
unbelieving people despair of God's mercy...*'"[43]

Once Imām Mūsā b. Ja'far, upon whom be peace, said to
Hishām b. Hakam:

"No one possesses true faith unless he both fears and
hopes. The fear and hope of such a one is grounded in
knowledge and awareness."[44]

The messengers of God and the leaders of religion who
have been the intermediaries between God and man always
based their summons on the combination of fear and hope. On
the one hand they gave their followers the glad tidings of
eternal bliss in exchange for obeying God's laws, and on the
other hand they warned them of the consequences of rebellion
against the laws of religion, namely punishment by God in the
hereafter.

The Glorious Qur'ān says concerning the Most Noble
Messenger:

"*We sent you for no purpose other than giving manking the glad
tidings of God's mercy and warning them of His punishment, but
most men are unaware of this truth*" (34:28).

* * * * *

By placing stress simultaneously on fear and hope, Islam
removes all kinds of fear which far from changing the reality of
man's situation simply weigh him down. It both liberates him

from fear of earthly factors and uproots from his being all kinds of false hope, so that he comes to place his reliance only on the eternal power of God.

Islam teaches that none of the factors that customarily induce fear in man possess in themselves the ability to cause benefit or harm, nor do they have the capacity to extend assistance; there is therefore no reason to fear them. Worthy of being feared is only that supreme and all-subduing power to the dominion of which all beings throughout the universe are subject. It is He Who gives and withholds.

The Qur'ān says:

"O Most Noble Messenger! Say 'Who is it that provides you with sustenance from the heavens and the earth? Who is it that gives you eyes and ears? Who is it that gives life to the dead and brings forth the living from the dead and the dead from the living? Who is it Whose command has bestowed order on the whole created universe?' They will say: 'God.' Then ask them why they do not fear God" (10: 31).

First material bounties and blessings are mentioned in this verse, and then the spiritual favors without which the material gifts would be pointless and empty of meaning. The verse then proceeds to mention two of the most remarkable phenomena in the world of being – life and death – which serve together, in a complex and mysterious way, to illustrate the infinite knowledge and power of the Creator. Then, after its evocation of the creation of all blessings and the mysteries of the universe, the verse mentions the guardian and administrator of all beings, and reminds short-sighted and misguided men that they should begin to fear God and His wrath, since they already acknowledge the disposition of all things to be in His hands.

* * * * *

Abū Dharr al-Ghifārī, the noble companion of the Messenger of God, upon whom and whose family be peace and blessings, whose heart overflowed with faith and sincere devotion to God, was troubled after the death of his son by anxiety over his fate and uncertainty whether he had truly joined the ranks of the blessed or been given a place among the damned.

Coming to his son's grave full of this painful anxiety, he placed his hands on the grave and said:

"O son, may God embrace you in His infinite mercy! While you were in this world you treated me well, and now that you have left this world, I declare myself well pleased with you. I swear by God that your death has not caused me any grief or distress, for I have no need of any but God. Were it not for the question of the hereafter and an eternal abode, I would be content to be in your place. It is anxiety over your fate for all eternity in the hereafter prevents me from mourning your death. I swear to God that I am weeping not out of sorrow at your death but because of the stages you must now traverse in the hereafter. Would that I knew what you have said and what you have been told after your death!"

He then turned toward God and addressed Him as follows:

"O God, I absolve him from whatever obligations to me as his father You placed upon him, so absolve him too from whatever obligations toward Yourself You placed upon him. Such generosity becomes You better than it becomes me."[45]

The Dissolution of Ties

One of the properties of resurrection is that it brings about the dissolution of all the relationships and mutual influences that mark the present order of the world. All causes and connections will be severed, so that things will no longer effect each other and creatures will no longer be subject to each other's influence. The only relationship that remains will be that of each object or being with its Creator; all other relationships will become utterly void.

This disssolution of ties and relationships will in reality demonstrate the essential nullity of all external causation; it is only the inner truth of all things that will be manifest on that day.

If the same causes and conditions that exist in the phenomenal world were to prevail on the plain of resurrection, the state of all created things would remain exactly the same as it is now and nothing would ever come to an end unless its very essence were transformed.

The Qur'ān depicts the scene of resurrection as follows:

"When the leaders of falsehood seek to dissociate themselves from their followers and behold punishment of God, all causes will be cut off from them and no relationship will remain" (2:166).

When the followers of the sinful lords of corruption begin to despair and cannot see even the smallest glimmer of hope for salvation, in their extreme wretchedness they turn for help to those false leaders whom they had followed so trustingly and unconditionally. But they will dissociate themselves from their followers and turn away from them. Then those followers will realize that all causes have ceased to operate and all doors have been closed. They will come to their senses and regret all the precious opportunities they have missed, all the vast possibilities they had for spiritual growth and perfection. They will be utterly dismayed, but regret and sorrow will be of no use. No path will open up before them to expiate past sins, nor will they have any time to engage in good deeds. They are doomed to remain for over in the pit they have dug for themselves, a pit that is now filled with torment and punishment.

Hishām b. Ḥakam asked Imām al-Ṣādiq, upon whom be peace:

"Will the spirit dissolve after it has quit the bodily frame, or will it remin in existence unchanging?"

The Imām answered: "Yes, the spirit will remain as it is until the trumpet of resurrection is sounded. Then all things will be voided. Neither sense will remain, nor anything to be sensed."[46]

So when all relationships of cause and effect are severed, the inner nature of all things will emerge. The manifest and the unseen realms will unite, and all the veils and obstacles that had hidden things from each other will vanish. The Qur'ān says in this connection:

"We have lifted from you the veil, so that this day your vision is sharp" (50:22).

On the day of resurrection none but God will have sovereignty or will.

The Qur'ān declares:

"On that day, none will be able to do anything for another; only God's will and command will have an effect" (82:19).

"On that day to whom shall belong the absolute ownership of the world? To God, the Unique and All-Powerful" (40:16).

Views of the Scholars

A question that arises here is whether the paradise and hellfire that are promised us already exist, or whether these realms of mercy and torment will be brought into being by the powerful will of God at the time of resurrection.

Muslim scholars have discussed this question for an extremely long time and put forth two views. The first is that paradise and hellfire do not presently exist; once the present order of the world comes to an end and is replaced by a new order, the infinite and everlasting power of God will create both heaven and hell.

However, the great majority of theologians state with great emphasis that the respective abodes of the pure and the sinful have already been created and therefore exist in the present. They cite numerous verses and narrations in support of this contention.

It is indeed necessary to draw inspiration from the text of the Qur'ān and from religious traditions in order to discover the truth of the matter, which is in fact what the majority of Islamic scholars proclaim it to be.

The Qur'ān says: *"Fear the fiery torment which has been prepared for the punishment of the unbelievers"* (3:131).

"Hasten to receive the forgiveness of your Lord, to the paradise which encompasses in its breadth all the heavens and the earth and which has already been prepared for the Godfearing" (3:133).

We can easily deduce from the word "prepared" the sense

of "created." In addition, there are other indications in Islamic sources confirming the correctness of this view.

The Qur'ān says the following in description of the ascension of the Most Noble Messenger, peace and blessings be upon him and his family:

"The Prophet saw once more the angel of revelation, near the lote-tree of the limit, at the place where eternal paradise is located" (53:13-15).

From these verses, too, it can be deduced that paradise already exists.

From other verses, however, verses which compare the breadth of paradise to the extent of the heavens and the earth, it can be deduced that paradise and hellfire are in a sense contained within the inner aspect of this world. On the day when the veil concealing the inner dimensions of things is removed and man gazes freely on the whole panorama of existence, he will clearly see the true aspect of paradise and hellfire immediately before him. However, under current circumstances, they lie beyond our perception. We can observe the earth and the heavenly bodies with our eyes, but our vision is not equal to the perception of the inner nature of this world; we cannot penetrate its depths. If we had a different mode of perception, we could see the inner dimension of this world. An analogy is provided by the fact that although we are surrounded by sound waves, our normal auditory faculties cannot pick them up unless aided by a transmitter. Once we have the receiver, we become aware of the waves. Despite this, some of the friends of God have been able to see paradise and hellfire while still in this world, with the truth-perceiving vision they had.

The created order is so vast and sublime that it is impossible for man to grasp all its various dimensions, despite the progress his knowledge has made. This being the case, the mere fact that the existence of paradise and hellfire have remained up to now beyond the reach of his direct knowledge does not permit him to deny their reality or to regard his denial as in way decisive. It is easy enough to negate and deny, and indeed many people do so, but no acceptable reason can be advanced for denying the existence of other worlds.

Has any outstanding scientific personality been able to draw on the accumulated resources of his specialization to examine all the aspects of creation and conclude, on the basis of precise experimentation, that paradise and hellfire are definitely non-existent?

Is it indeed possible for anyone even to make such an attempt, and is it conceivable that such a claim would have any basis in science?

Although man is continually engaged in the conquest of new realms, we know that the universe is so vast that if the sound waves which circle the globe in seven seconds were to traverse the whole universe at the same speed, it would take a hundred million years!

The amount of awareness and knowledge that we presently possess is the product of the augmentation of man's knowledge with each succeeding generation. It is quite probable that in the vast ocean of the cosmos great worlds exist the structure of which totally escapes our awareness; there is no reason for absolutely denying their existence.

Einstein said:

"The great riddle of creation remains insoluble. We cannot even be sure that it will ever be solved. What we have been able to read so far in the book of nature has taught us many things, but we know that in contrast to the sentences we have able to read and understand, we are still far removed from being decipher everything. Is indeed such a total decipherment possible?"[47]

Considering all this, the categorical denial of the present existence of both paradise and hellfire lacks all logical justification.

In addition, once the carpet of time is rolled up and motion itself is thereby brought to an end, temporal relationships which permit "before" and "after" to be established will no longer exist.

Lesson Fifteen
Compensating for Our Sins

In just the same way that numerous bodily sicknesses can be cured, the spirit can be cured of its afflictions. Islam has pointed the way to the cure by summoning man to repentance and calling on him to return to piety, virtue, and true happiness; it promises him in return the favor and mercy of God.

The messengers of God, whose proud lives were never penetrated by any element of sin, would always invite sinners to seek God's forgiveness and encourage them to place their hopes in His mercy, for His kindness and compassion toward His believing servants are such that He would never abandon them in the dark pit of disobedience and sin. On the contrary, He invites all men to return to Him, and it is up to us to answer His call and thus act to attain our salvation.

God's acceptance of repentance indicates a particular worthiness in man to receive God's mercy, a worthiness which causes the gates of forgiveness to remain open before sinners. They have the opportunity to express contrition and shame before God over their dark past and to abandon and attempt to make up for the evil they have committed. If they do this, all their misfortune will be turned to good fortune, and all their darkness to light.

When the penitent thus prepare themselves to obey divine command and begin to purify their spirits, the black pages of sin are removed from the record of their deeds and only the golden pages of virtue and goodness remain. This is the meaning of God's words: *"Then God will transform their evil works into good works, for He is Forgiving and Merciful"* (25:70).

To despair of forgiveness and the cleansing of the soul, to have the constant awareness of sin and pollution, is a tormenting pain that is full of danger both for the person of the sinner and for the society in which he lives.

The message of repentance is an important factor in cleansing the soul and preparing man for the rest of his life. Where the promise implicit in repentance not to be given to sinners, were they not to have the slightest hope of salvation, no sinner would ever begin to think of reforming himself halfway through his life; indeed, the record of his deeds would grow blacker day by day and he would engage freely in corruption and sin until the end of his life.

When a believer in God's unity commits a sin, it leaves a dark imprint on his heart, for while committing the sin he has forgotten that God Almighty is watching over him, with His infinite splendor and sublimity, and thus cut himself off from Him. But by remembering God anew, he returns to awareness of Him; in his belief that nothing can stand in the way of the favors that God decrees and that the door of His mercy is always open for His servants, He hastens to receive God's forgivess.

* * * * *

Anyone who is concerned with his eternal welfare will immediately feel the burden of disobedience and pollution weighing heavily on him once he allows himself to be drawn by passion and ignorance toward the precipice of sin and rebellion against divine command. He will make haste immediately to seek God's forgiveness and implore God for His mercy and pardon.

Imām al-Sajjād, upon whom be peace, thus addresses God in the prayer of Abū Hamza:

"O God, when I was drawn to sinning and disobeying you, I did not sin in denial of Your Lordship, nor did I act thus because I took Your commands lightly. I did not belittle Your punishment, nor did I disregard Your threat of requital. Sin presented itself before me, my concupiscent soul deluded me, and passion prevailed over me."

But if a person immerses himself in all the varieties of sin without any awareness of the ugliness of what he is doing, firmly advancing on the path of corruption until the travails of death overtake him, this means that he is totally heedless of the consequences of his acts; any belated repentance on his part will not be accepted.

It is obvious that when a sinner comes to the threshold of death and the veils are removed from before him, in such a way that the hereafter become sensorily visible to him, he will regret his evil deeds. His state will be comparable to that of a condemned criminal who finally repents of his crime when he lays eyes on the gallows that await him. Such fruitless regret cannot be regarded as a virtue or cause for pride; it does not mark a spiritual reformation, and is not an acceptable form of repentance.

The Noble Qur'ān clearly states: "*The one who continues to sin until he witnesses death and then begins to experience regret, saying, 'Now I repent' — the repentance of such a one will not be accepted*" (4:18).

Once someone said in the presence of the Commander of the Faithful, upon whom be peace, in an offhand and careless fashion, "I seek the forgiveness of God." The Imām said to him: "May your mother weep for you! Do you know what it is to seek the forgiveness of God? Seeking forgiveness of God is the station of those of high rank. It appears to be but a word, but it includes six aspects. The first is regret for what has been done; the second is firm resolve to abandon sinning in future; the third is restoring to others whatever rights of theirs you may have usurped, in such a way that when you meet your Creator they will have no claim in you; the fourth is that you perform whatever obligatory acts of worship you may have neglected; the fifth is that you cleanse with the tears of regret the illicit flesh that grew on your body while you were sinning; and the sixth is that just as you tasted the pleasure of sin and disobedience, you now taste the hardship and rigor of worship and obedience. Only when you have completed all of these six may you say, 'I seek forgiveness of God.'"[48]

The Qur'ān says concerning the repentance of the usurers: "*If you do not abandon usury, be aware that you are engaged in war against God and His Messenger. But if you truly regret your practice and repent of it, then the original sum shall be yours; no wrong shall be done to you, nor will you have wronged others. If one of your debtors is indigent, grant him a respite until he is able to pay; and if you forgive him his debt by way of charity, this will be better for you, if you are aware of your own true interest*" (2:279-280).

The Qur'ān pronounces the repentance of the usurer to be a true repentance only if he renounces the interest that is due him and simply reclaims the original sum; in such a case, neither will he have wronged anyone nor will he have been wronged himself.

The Qur'ān then adds that it is better for the lender to give a respite to the borrower, enabling him to obtain the money needed for repaying the debt. If the lender forgives the debt, it will be still better, the reason for this being that it is usually dire need that forces people into debt. This act of renunciation will have the effect of softening the heart that had been made merciless and hard by the practice of usury, and in addition the resentment and hatred that had accumulated in the borrower will be changed into liking and approval. Love will thus have displaced enmity.

The Advantages Bestowed by Repentance

To confess to one's sins, to repent and to seek God's forgiveness, not only does not reduce a person's value in the eyes of God; it increases his standing with Him. It cleanses his soul of the dark stains of sin and enables him, with God's help, to make up for his past errors and begin to acquire virtue, and to play the role for which he was created. Once an intelligent believer in God's unity became aware of the darkness of sin within his own being, he will begin seeking for a way to remedy matters. Where else he might turn for help if not to the source of all mercy and good?

The Qur'ān says:

"The virtuous are those who whenever they commit an improper act or transgress against themselves remember God, and repent and seek forgiveness from Him. None but God can forgive the sins of His creatures. The virtuous are those who do not persist in sin, for they are aware of the ugliness of disobedience" (3:135).

The Qur'ān describes as follows the truly penitent who are enveloped in the grace and forgiveness of God:

"God accepts the repentance of those who have sinned in ignorance and who realizing the ugliness of their deed swiftly turn toward Him in repentance" (3:16).

The Qur'ān similarly instructs those who are concerned for their salvation to come to their senses by turning to God in repentance and reforming their conduct.

"O believers, turn toward God, all of you, in repentance, in hope of attaining success and salvation" (24:31).

It is important that whenever man falls into the pit of sin, he should immediately feel polluted by his act of rebellion against God, and that he move to prevent his heart from being blackened by the repetition of sin and, in fact, receiving the stamp of perdition.

Perceiving the ugliness of his deeds, the sinner begins immediately to lament and to implore God for forgiveness. True repentance can take place only through turning to God, striving to advance continuously on the path of knowledge and faith, and compensating for past error.

God commands His servants to engage in sincere repentance and the definitive renunciation of sin in order to efface the effects of their sinning. Only thus can they truly purge themselves of their offenses, with a comprehensive repentance and contrition that laying firm hold of the heart cures it. Any seeking of forgiveness that falls short of this will be purely verbal.

This is God's command:

"O believers, turn toward God in sincere repentance, and it may

be that God will veil and efface your sins" (66:8).

Traditions confirm for us that a sincere repentance is one that includes the firm resolve not to resume sinning.

* * * * *

The Commander of the Faithful, upon whom be peace, regarded the avoidance of contamination by sin as an important factor in attaining nobility and dignity of character. For he said: "Whoever claims nobility and dignity for his person will not abase it with vice and sin."[49]

Man who is constantly exposed in the life of this world to the danger of sin should then always be careful not to approach that forbidden zone. At the same time, the greater becomes his share of faith, the loftier and purer his deeds will become.

Now is the time to seek a remedy for sin and to make up for past misdeeds; we cannot wait, for the opportunity to repent may pass us by.

The Commander of the Faithful, upon whom be peace, warns us as follows:

"O servants of God, prepare yourselves now to work good. For your tongues suffer no impediment, your bodies are sound, and limbs are obedient. The field of action is open before all of you."[50]

Imām al-Ṣādiq, peace be upon him, similarly said:

"The life of man does not amount to more than an instant. What is past is now non-existent; you do not feel its pleasure or pain. As for what is yet to come, you do not know what it is.

"The true and precious capital of your life are those few instants you presently enjoy. Master, then, your soul, and strive to redeem yourself and attain salvation; be steadfast in enduring the rigor of worshipping God and obeying His commandments; and preserve your self from the pollution of sin and disobedience to God."[51]

The Most Noble Messenger, peace and blessings be upon him and his family, said:

"O servants of God, you are like the sick, and the Creator

of the world is like a physician. The interest and welfare of the sick lie in those things that the physician does in accordance with his knowledge, not in those things that the sick crave for. Surrender to God's commands in order to join the ranks of the saved."[52]

Imām al-Ṣādiq, upon whom be peace, said:

"Restrain your soul from what harms it before death overtakes you. Strive to keep your soul free in just the same way that you strive to earn your livelihood. For your soul is hostage to your deeds, and only your efforts can set it free."[53]

The Commander of the Faithful, upon whom be peace, said"

"Tame your rebellious and transgressing soul by abandoning the habit of sin; compel it to obey God's commands; and impose on it the burden of compensating for its violations. Then adorn it with moral and spiritual virtues and keep it free from the pollution of sin."[54]

We must implore God to treat us not in accordance with His justice but in accordance with His kindness and mercy, for if He were to withhold from us His favor and forgiveness, we would never attain salvation and happiness.

Imām al-Sajjād, upon whom be peace, addressed God as follows:

"O God, if You wish, forgive us by virtue of Your kindness, and if You wish, punish us by virtue of Your justice. Then show us Your favor, envelop us in Your pardon, and keep us safe in Your refuge from all torment. You know well that We cannot endure Your justice or withstand the chastisement that we merit; none can attain salvation except through Your forgiveness and generosity.

"When we sinned against You, Satan rejoiced; now that we have severed our links with him and turned toward You, do not abandon us or drive us away."[55]

Lesson Sixteen
Man's Situation in the Intermediate Realm

The present existence of an intermediate realm and of separate destinations there for the virtuous and the wicked is a well-founded religious belief. There can be no doubt that after death the spirits of men – the only element within them that is truly essential – are transferred to the vast expanse of the non-material world.

Just as the spirit appears in man's body and material form after it has been fashioned to completion, the spirit retains its attachment to the body as long as the body retains the capacity for a harmonious relation with the spirit. Once this capacity vanishes as a result of external factors so that the union of spirit and body is sundered, the spirit separates from the body and pursues its existence under a different order and set of conditions.

What we mean by this order is the intermediate realm, the first stage reached by man after his migration from the world. He pauses there in the course of his journey to the meeting with God. He enters a realm with its own specific characteristics and properties, remaining there until the coming of resurrection.

A further change then brings about the transformation of the intermediate realm, and man enters the plain of resurrection, the next stage in his journey toward God.

A limit or boundary separating two things is called *barzakh* in Arabic, which explains why the intermediate realm that separates the temporary and evanescent life of this world from the eternal life of the hereafter is also called *barzakh*. Life there is characterized by the liberation of the spirit from the fetters of the material body. The spirit is no longer harassed by passion and instinct, and thanks to the absence of time and space, the horizons of man's vision are vastly enlarged. In just the same way that there is no question of time or space in the world of dreams, in the intermediate realm, too, man can observe and examine everything in a single instant.

The Qur'ān says: "*The intermediate realm extends from now until the time of resurrection*" (23: 100).

In the same connection, the Qur'ān describes the state of the martyrs after their death:

"*Do not imagine those who have been killed in God's path to be dead; rather they are alive and receive sustenance in the presence of their Lord*" (3: 169).

The verse refers, of couse, to willingness to defend the sanctity of Islam and the Qur'ān, to the virtue of heroically resisting the unbelievers and atheists even to the point of attaining martyrdom. This is the highest point the believer can reach: the desire to sacrifice himself for the sake of his pure goals and thereby to join the caravan of martyrs.

He regards it as a great duty to guard God's religion and to strive for the implementation of the commands of the Qur'ān, and he therefore exerts great effort to secure the security and survival of the religion of God. Such a protector of the true faith must necessarily begin by purifying himself and avoiding all kinds of pollution by sin and disobedience to God. It is only then that he may properly return his soul – the loftiest trust which he has been given – to God, its true owner, while fighting for the sake of His religion. He will then receive the reward of life everlasting in the company of God's chosen elite.

The Qur'ān says:

"*God has bought the properties and souls of the believers in exchange for paradise. They are to strive in the path of God, destroying the enemies of religion or themselves being killed. This is a firm promise of God, binding upon Him, contained in the Torah, the Gospels and the Qur'ān, and who is more faithful to his promises than God? O believers, rejoice in this transaction, for it truly guarantees great happiness"* (9:111).

The Qur'ān also draws attention to the punishment being suffered before the occurrence of resurrection by those bound for hellfire:

"Hellfire has already encompassed the unbelievers" (9:49).

After death, the spirits of the virtuous will rejoice in liberation from the constricting cage of this world, they will delight in their ability to roam freely through the infinite. Life on the earthly plane is concerned only with the limited amount of matter that is visible on the surface of the earth. By contrast, the spirits of the virtuous know no limitation of space or time as they continue their upward ascent. Each in accordance with its rank advances joyfully to its specific station and degree, and everywhere it enjoys unhindered access. The eyes of the blessed witness pure and uncontaminated sources of eternal beauty in comparison with which the beauties of this world are slight and inconsequential.

The spirit is no longer subject to the limits imposed on it by a weary, heavy body; it is not accompanied by the broken and suffering countenace of old age.

Nothing exists here for the righteous servants of God except beauty, luminosity, love, familiarity and effection, and pure, sincere friendship with the servants and friends of God.

The Qur'ān promises those who have made obedience to divine command their guiding principle in this world that they shall enjoy the company and fellowship of God's chosen elite.

The companionship of those upon whom God has bestowed His blessings in full measure is indeed a source of great pride for the virtuous.

This is the promise contained in the Qur'ān:

"Those who obey the commands of God and His Messenger shall be resurrected together with, and enjoy the company of, those upon whom God has bestowed His kindness and favor in full measure — the prophets, the sincere devotees, the martyrs and the righteous. What

noble and precious companions they are!" (4:64).

It should be remarked, of course, that enjoying the company of God's chosen elite does not imply equality with them in terms of spiritual station and degree. While being in close contact with them, the virtuous will enjoy God's favor and blessings to an extent commensurate with their own ranks and degrees of closeness to God. Not everyone will enjoy an equal share, in just the same way that not everyone attains the same degree of ascent.

* * * * *

One of the companions of Imām al-Ṣādiq, upon whom be peace, relates that he once posed him the following question:

"O descendant of God's Messenger! When the true believer finds himself on the threshold of death, is he grieved by the taking of his soul?"

The Imām answered:

"Never! When the messenger of death comes to take his spirit, he is at first distraught. But then the angel consoles him and says: 'O friens of God, do not distress yourself. I swear by the Lord Who sent Muḥammad as His Messenger that we will treat you more kindly and gently than your father. Open your eyes and look at us.'

"Then the Messenger of God and the other preceptors of religion will appear before him, and the angel entrusted with the task of taking his soul will say to him: 'This is the Prophet and the leaders of religion who will be your friends and companions.'

"He will then open his eyes partly, and hear God calling him as follows:

"'O soul that has found tranquillity in the protection of Muḥammad and his pure family, now return to your Lord. You have accepted as truth the authority of the Imāms, and because of this you are now happy. Be certain that you have also earned thereby the pleasure of your Lord. Come now and be the companion of My chosen elite, and take up the abode that has been prepared for you in paradise everlasting.'

"Nothing could be more desirable for the believer at that moment than for his soul to take flight and receive all that it has been promised."[56]

The Painful State of the Impure

The spirits of the impure are meanwhile caught up in terrible darkness and gloom. Overwhelmed by misery and disaster, they mourn their lives of sin. Realizing that neither their relatives nor the material wealth they accumulated can do anything to deliver them, they torment themselves in their wretchedness.

Still more terrible than their fate is that of cruel, vicious and arrogant tyrants. The sighs and laments of their oppressed victims are like so many daggers plunged in their hearts. The specter of those whom they have wronged assaults them mercilessly with constant blame and reproach, augmenting constantly the pain and misery they suffer.

The vision of these spectacles of terror is like a tormenting flame consuming the heart of the criminal.

The Qur'ān depicts the catastrophic destiny of aggressive tyrants as follows:

"*They will be brought to the fire every morning and evening, and the descendants of Pharaoh will be punished most severely*" (40:46).

They will then recall vividly the repeated warnings of the prophets and men of religion who told them of the disasters that awaited them. They will begin to blame themselves for not following the commands of the prophets and not heeding their kindly advice, for had they done so, they would not have cast themselves into perdition.

In the course of the Battle of Badr, some of the leaders of Quraysh were killed and their bodies were thrown in a pit. After the victory of the Muslim army, the Most Noble Messenger, peace and blessings be upon him and his family, leaned over the edge of the pit and addressed them as follows:

"We have attained all that God promised us; are you now convinced of the truth of God's promises?"

Some of the companions then said: "O Messenger of God,

you are talking to the dead, to bodies that have been thrown into a pit; do they understand anything of what you say?"

The Prophet answered them: "They hear more clearly than you do."[57]

One of the companions of the Commander of the Faithful, upon whom be peace, said:

"Once I left Kūfa in the company of the Imām. He stopped in the cemetery at Wādī al-Salām, standing there like someone about to address a gathering. I remained there standing with the Imām until I grew tired and sat down. Another long time passed, and I grew tired of sitting. So I stood up again and remained standing until once again I grew tired and sat down. Finally, I arose once more, and said to the Commander of the Faithful: 'I fear for you, seeing you standing so long; rest a little.' I then spread out my cloak on the ground for the Imām to sit down. He said: 'O Ḥabba! I am standing here engaged in conversation with the believers.' I then asked him: 'Do they also engage in conversation with each other?' 'Yes,' he said. 'Once the veil is lifted you will see them gathered in circles conversing with each other.' I said: 'Are you speaking of their bodies or their spirits?' 'Their spirits,' he answered."[58]

From this narrative it can be deduced that the spirit does not entirely sever its relations with the body. It is true that after the death and the cutting of the link between the spirit and the body, the spirit leaves for a different realm. However, on account of the union that existed between them in this world, some weak connection persists, in the form of a certain affinity. On account of this affinity and its former union with the body, the spirit is oriented toward the remains of the body in way that it is not oriented to anything else.

Islam has laid down certain instructions relating to the body after death. The reason for them is the continuing affinity of the spirit for the body and the trials and turmoil the spirit encounters in the unfamiliar realm of the *barzakh*, governed as it is by new principles and criteria.

In the intermediate realm men encounter each other in bodily forms specific to that realm. The pure and virtuous are gathered together, in groups determined by their spiritual rank and degree. The unbelievers and the evil also find themselves in each other's company. The dealings and relations of the pious with each other are based on familiarity, intimacy, and pure love, and thus anticipate the states of paradise. By contrast, the relations of the unbelievers with each other will inevitably partake of the character of hellfire; mutual enmity, disgust and envy will prevail among them.

It is self-evident that since all things will be determined in the intermediate realm by the particular laws and criteria that prevail there, the companionship and conversation of the blessed and the damned, as well as the enjoyment of divine bounties by the former and the experience of punishment by the latter, will also be marked by the characteristics of that realm.

Although the bodies of men in the intermediate realm will in general resemble the bodily form they had in this world, certain differences will also be apparent, because every quality and attribute will take on an external form commensurate with its inner nature. Thus the spiritual light or darkness found within individuals will become clearly visible in their faces.

Ibrāhīm b. Isḥāq recounts that he asked Imām al-Ṣādiq, upon whom be peace: "Where are the souls of the believers?" He answered: "The spirits of the believers are lodged in paradise, where they are given to eat and to drink. They see and visit each other, and they say, 'O Lord, bring about resurrection so that what You have promised us may be fulfilled.'"

Ibrāhīm next asked: "Where are the spirits of the unbelievers?" He answered: "Their place is in the fire, where they are compelled to eat the food of the fire and to drink its drink. They see each other and meet each other and they say, 'O God, do not bring about resurrection lest that which You promised us be fulfilled.'"[59]

Abū Baṣīr relates that the question of the spirits of the believers and the Godfearing was once being discussed in the presence of Imām al-Sādiq, upon whom be peace. The Imām said: "The spirits of the believers meet each other." I asked: "Do they indeed meet each other?" He replied: "Yes, and they talk to each other and recognise each other; when you see someone there, you will say, 'This is so-and-so.'"[60]

Those living in the intermediate realm can even establish contact with the material world and its inhabitants. By virtue of the inner capacities they developed and the deeds they performed while still in the world, they can acquire information of a general kind about their relatives and friends to the degree that is permitted by the special circumstances of the intermediate realm.

The situation of people in the intermediate realm naturally differs from one person to the next. In a sense, everyone there has his own world, the nature of which is determined by the conduct he exhibited in this world; not all the dwellers in the intermediate realm can communicate uniformly with this world and its people. The degree to which an individual may have awareness of the material world and communicate with it depends on the spiritual rank and degree of development he has attained.

Those who worship and fear God have, therefore, better and more extensive capacity for gaining awareness of the material world. Within the limits set by the particular circumstances of the intermediate realm and depending on God's permission, they can be present wherever they wish, simply through willing it and turning themselves in the proper direction. As for the errant and sinful, their communication with the world serves simply to increase their regret and torment.

Imām al-Ṣādiq, upon whom be peace, says:

"The believer visits his dear ones and relatives, and he sees what he loves, while whatever he dislikes is concealed from him. The unbeliever also visits his dear ones and relatives, but he sees what he hates and dislikes, while whatever he loves is concealed from him.

"Among the believers are those for whom Friday is a day of visiting, and there also those the balance of whose deeds permits them to see them."[61]

Someone relates that he asked the Commander of the Faithful, upon whom be peace, whether the dead are able to visit their relatives. He answered that they are, whereupon the questioner asked: "When and how often?" He answered: "Every week, every month, or every year, depending of spiritual rank and capacity."[62]

The Qur'ān speaks in the following terms of the constant torment and punishment that are administered to the evil and corrupt in the intermediate realm:

"They are brought to the fire every morning and evening, and the descendants of the Pharaoh shall be brough forth on the day of resurrection with the severest torment" (40:46).

It is obvious that this verse must refer to the intermediate realm, not to resurrection, for after resurrection there will be neither morning nor evening.

The Qur'ān similarly says of the blessed:

"Provision shall be brought to them every morning and evening" (19:62).

This verse also contains mention of morning and evening, the reference being probably to the morning and evening of the intermediate realm which follow upon the morning and evening of this world. It cannot refer to paradise, because the Qur'ān says:

"There (in paradise) they shall not see the sun nor experience severe cold" (76:13).

"The people of paradise shall have on that day a better abode and the fairest of places for repose" (25:24).

In the second of these two verses, the word *maqīl* which we have translated as "place of repose" is of particular interest because it refers to a nap taken before noon. It is true that sleep in the intermediate realm cannot resemble exactly sleep in this world, but it is nonetheless different from what will prevail after resurrection, namely eternal wakefulness. This is indeed one reason why people are described as *qiyām* — "awake" or "alert" on the day of resurrection.

The degree of life possessed by those in the intermediate

realm is, in some sense, fuller than the life of this world, which may be what is suggested by this tradition: "People are asleep, and when they die they wake up."[63]

This refers to the fact that when a person goes to sleep, his senses and perceptions are weakened; he can almost be said to be half-alive. When he awakens, he regains a full measure of life. Likewise, the degree of life man enjoys in this world is less than which awaits him in the intermediate realm; when he is transferred to that realm, his degree of life is enhanced.

al-Ghazālī says:

"When we are asleep we witness a world in which we do not imagine that we are asleep. This particular state is only a part of the total scheme of our life, the totality being represented by our waking state, and indeed, as soon as we wake up, we realize that our state while asleep represented only a part of our life, not the whole.

"This being the case, why should our present life not be like a period spent asleep in relation to the hereafter? Our firm belief that our present life in this world is equivalent to life as such is just like the supposition of the sleeper.

"When we wake up, we say that we understand we were sleeping and dreaming; whatever we experienced had no reality. By this we mean that our sleep was only part of the greater reality which is constituted by our waking state, for sleep is in itself a reality. Likewise, the life of this world is real in and of itself, but compared with the more expansive life that awaits us, it counts as a dream."[64]

In the intermediate realm, the spirits of men pursue their lives according to the different degrees of consciousness that their belief and awareness have made possible for them. Since life there is not subject to the laws of matter, following instead its own particular criteria, its conditions must naturally be different from those of our present life. However, since man's perceptions are much sharpened in the intermediate realm, the spiritual torment and pleasure which he undergoes there escape our present powers of description.

The fruit of man's deeds becomes tangible for him in the

intermediate realm. Those who have never had the good fortune of doing good deeds wish to return to the world to make up for their past. The Qur'ān says:

"Spend in the path of God a part of the sustenance We have bestowed on you, before death overtakes you. Then the sinner will say, 'O Lord, if You were to grant me a respite and postpone my death a little, I would certainly do good and become one of the virtuous'" (63:10).

As for the righteous and pious, they will joyously exclaim in the intermediate world:

"Would that our relatives and kin knew how God has forgiven us and bestowed mercy and favor upon us" (36:26-27).

One of the characteristics of the intermediate realm is that both its pleasures and torments are temporary, being brought to an end when resurrection begins.

Certain verses of the Qur'ān refer to the state of people intermediate between belief and unbelief – i.e., those who were deprived by various circumstances or hardships of the opportunity of learning about Islam or investigating its truth, or were prevented from migrating from one land to another.

It is probable that such persons, if they have not committed any crimes, will be enveloped in God's mercy and forgiveness on the day of resurrection. In the intermediate realm, neither will they be punished nor will they enjoy blessings; they will simply wait for their destiny to be clarified.

The disquiet they endure will be comparable to that of prisoners whose case is still under investigation and whose future is unclear.

The Qur'ān says:

"Those who have wronged themselves in this world will be asked by the angels when they die what they have done. They will say, 'We were weak and oppressed and unable to move.' Then the angels will ask, 'Was God's earth not wide enough for you to travel in it (so that you might hasten from the land of ignorance to that of faith and knowledge)?' The abode of these evildoers shall be hellfire; how evil and terrible an abode! Excepted from this shall be those men, women and children who were indeed unable to act or to move; they could not flee

and they had no path of escape. It may be that God will forgive and show mercy to them, for He is Merciful and Pardoning" (4:97-99).

This verse clearly relates to the intermediate realm, because after resurrection the status and destiny of everyone is made clear.

* * * * *

In reality, then, the intermediate realm represents a small portion of the reward or punishment that man will receive after resurrection; it is like a window through which one can glimpse the ultimate outcome of his affair.

There are numerous traditions concerning the state of the Godfearing in the intermediate realm. They state clearly that although the Godfearing do not yet enter paradise, a gate to paradise is opened before them permitting them to glimpse the abode that awaits them and feel the pleasant breezes that blow there.

Tolstoy, the great Russian author, writes:

O God, it is You alone Who can open a door on the world of mercy to Your servant who lies buried beneath the ground.

Out of all these bones lying here, gradually rotting, Which belong to a king, and which to a beggar? Which belong to a judge, and which to a soldier? Which belong to a pious man who has bought heaven for himself, and which to a sinner, who has been driven away from the kingdom of heaven? Whatever we see is darkness, visions and ghosts – O God, it is only at the threshold of Your throne, only in Your heavens that we may find a path leading to tranquillity and salvation.

On the day that nothing remains of our earthly form except a pitiful handful of dust and all the brilliance of our life has been buried in the black earth, it is You alone Who can open a door on the world of mercy to Your servant who lies buried beneath the ground.[65]

The first reality that presents itself to man the moment he dies and embarks on a new life is the voiding of all the customs, conventions and norms that governed his worldly life. All outward causation and instrumentality will come to an end, and man will enter a realm that is utterly empty of all the varied phenomena found in this world. All the aims and pursuits he has followed throughout his life will turn into a mirage.

The Qur'ān says:

"If you were to see catastrophic misery of the oppressors when they are caught in the throes of death! The angels lift their powerful hands to seize their souls, telling them, 'Give up now your souls. Today you shall suffer torment and humiliation because you spoke lyingly of God and refused in your arrogance to accept His signs.' Certainly you will return to Us, one by one, just as We first created you. You will leave behind all the property and wealth We bestowed on you (this being the cause of your arrogance), and all the intermediaries and intercessors you thought that you had shall be destroyed and separated from you" (6:93-94).

"If you speak truly when you say there is no resurrection, why is it that when you stand at the bedside of the dying, as their souls rise in their throats, at a time when We are closer to them than you are (although you do not realize this) — why is it that then, if everything is indeed in your hands or the hands of nature, you do not return their souls to their bodies? If the one who dies is among those who have drawn nigh to God, their place is in eternal rest and repose. If he is from among the Companions of the Right, then give glad tidings that he is safe. If he is from among the deniers and misguided, then his share shall be the boiling water and his abode shall be hellfire. All of this is truth, concerning which there is no doubt" (56:83-95).

Commenting on the part of the verse that refers to *"those who have drawn nigh to God,"* Imām al-Ṣādiq, upon whom be peace, says that it refers to the intermediate realm, while *"eternal rest and repose"* refers to paradise.[66]

Imām al-Ṣādiq also said: "By God, I fear for you in the intermediate realm." 'Amr b. Yazīd then asked him: "What is the intermediate realm?" He answered: "The tomb in which you will stay until the day of resurrection."[67]

Man puts his trust in two things in this life. First, the

worldly goods of which he imagines himself to be the owner
and which he regards as the means for attaining his wishes and
desires. Second, those persons without whose help and
influence he thinks himself incapable of fulfilling his needs –
powerful friends, relatives and the like. The Qur'ān stresses
that both of these pass away and have no ultimate validity.
Once man finds himself on the threshold of death, he is
compelled to sever all material attachments, and with a belated
realism that is forced upon him, he understands the emptiness
of everything in which he had placed his trust.

He even wishes for the impossible – to return and warn
his relatives not to do anything which might plunge them into
the same whirlpool of eternal wretchedness as himself.

The Most Noble Messenger, peace and blessings be upon
him and his family, is reported to have said:

"The spirit of the dead will cry out after death: 'O family
and offspring! Take care not to be deceived by the world as it
deceived and misled me. I accumulated wealth, making no
distinction between the licit and the illicit, in the end leaving it
behind for others to enjoy; all that remains for me is misery.
Take care to avoid what has befallen me.'"[68]

Imām al-Hādī, upon whom be peace, compared the world
to a marketplace when he said: "The world is a market in which
some people profit and others lose."[69]

The Qur'ān likewise summons men to engage in a
profitable trade in the market of this world:

"*O believers, shall I guide you to a trade which shall free you
from painful torment in the hereafter? Believe in God and His
Messenger and struggle in God's path with your property and your
person*" (61:10-11).

One of the companions of Imām al-Ṣādiq, upon whom be
peace, said: "I asked the Imām to counsel me. He answered:
'Make provision for your journey, and make ready the goods
that you will need on your voyage. Take all the necessary
measures youself, and do not instruct another after the end of
your life to send on what you need.'"[70]

The Commander of the Faithful, upon whom be peace,

said:

"The world is a transient abode, not a permanent dwelling. People in this world are of two kinds: those who have sold themselves, who have deviated from the path of truth and are advancing toward perdition; and those who have bought themselves, who have chosen the path of salvation and liberated themselves."[71]

Lesson Seventeen
The Criteria by Which
Our Deeds will be Judged

Let us now examine how our deeds will be judged and weighed after resurrection. As we have previously remarked, the mental pictures we form of scenes that have no precedent in our lives nor bear any similarity to it will necessarily be imaginary; they will be unable to advance us to the direct perception of the reality in question.

It would be futile were one to expect to trace out in his mind something of the nature and characteristics of the hereafter. For we are now confined in the prison of the world and a clear boundary has been drawn between us and the next world; how might we perceive the splendor and profundity and the perfection of the life that awaits us there? A finite being subject to change cannot possibly conceive an accurate notion of the eternal.

When, therefore, we speak of accounting and judgement in the hereafter, it should not be imagined that this corresponds precisely to the drawing up of dossiers and the investigations and trials that take place in this world. The true nature of the matter is hidden in obscurity, and whatever image we form of it ought to be forgotten.

Those who follow the path of truth know that when we speak of a world which is utterly different from the present one and the means that will be applied there to judge men's deeds with respect to good and evil, it should not be thought that men will be faced with some prosecutor who carefully weighs their deeds in some huge scale, and that then they are given the opportunity to defend themselves before the court issues its verdict for implementation by the executive branch. The concept of the scale or the balance presented in the Qur'ān is infinitely more comprehensive than what is implied by this picture. Thus God says:

"*He raised the heavens and He placed in all things a balance and means of accounting*" (55:7).

"*At the time of resurrection, We shall set up the scales of justice, and none will be wronged on that day. Everyone will be requited in accordance with his deeds. We shall take into reckoning the smallest of deeds, even if it be no greater than a mustard grain, for it is We who shall call them to account*" (21:47).

"*The day of resurrection is in truth the day on which deeds shall be weighed. Those whose good deeds weigh heavy in the balance shall be saved and those whose deeds are slight are those who have wronged themselves by transgressing against the signs and messengers of God*" (7:8-9).

These verses point out that those who have squandered the capital of their existence will suffer eternal and irredeemable loss, for the loss that results in the corruption of the very essence of man's being is the greatest of all losses and no compensation can be made for it.

It should be remembered that we cannot always apply the criteria with which we are familiar to understanding the words of the Qur'ān; we must seek to understand the concepts that underlie them and the results to which they give rise. Moreover, the words to which we have recourse in attempting to explain matters are inevitably defective.

* * * * *

Thanks to the progress of science, man has discovered means for measuring air and blood, the temperature of the body, and electrical currents. However, he does not possess means for measuring the motives and intentions of men's deeds or their good and their evil. It is in the hereafter that means exist for the measurement and assessment of such matters.

Precise criteria and means of measurement exist there for assessing the spiritual and moral dimensions of men's deeds, permitting a division of them into good and evil. In our present circumstances we are unaware of the exact nature of those means, for our knowledge of the mutable world in which we live is derived from the experiences we derived from it. The other world possesses a content and characteristics which are beyond our capacity to perceive directly or even to guess; the possibility of experiencing it is totally excluded.

Hishām relates that he asked Imām al-Ṣādiq, upon whom be peace, the meaning of the verse, "*At the time of resurrection, We shall set up the scales of justice*" (21:47).

The Imām replied: "The prophets and the legatees are the scales."[72]

What he meant by this was that everyone can measure his own weight and value by comparing his faith and his deeds to theirs.

Even in the present world, there are pure, virtuous and Godfearing persons who represent a criterion of measurement. In this world, however, many realities are hidden; on the day of resurrection, which is the day on which inner realities will become manifest, the nature of the scales will also become apparent. If the word "scales" is in the plural in the Qur'ān, this is because the friends of God, the true exemplars of humanity who furnish the measure against whom all persons should be measured, are several.

A good act has two dimensions, one being its outward effect and the other its relationship to the one who performs it. When examined with respect to the first dimension, its external beneficial effect, the act is seen to have "practical goodness." When is examined with respect to the second dimension, the spiritual causes that gave rise to it, it is seen to have a "goodness of agent."

Islam thus establishes criteria for the deeds and conduct of man. Not every deed is acceptable; a deed acquires moral value only when it arises from a pure motive. It is basing one's choices and acts on pure motives, pleasing to God, that enables man to develop himself morally, and it is according to those motives that he is judged.

Sometimes man bows his head in submission to the urgings of his instinctual self acts accordingly. On other occasions he is heedful of God, the source of all being, and reins in his self, satisfied with what God has given him. In the former case he will have permitted the negative dimensions of his nature to flourish, and in the latter case he will have contributed to the growth of his positive and truly human dimensions.

How might these two types of motivation be regarded as equal: one leading to a deed characterized by pure spirituality, and the other to a deed tainted with hypocrisy and deceit?

Those who are heedful of God never forget that God watches vigilantly over their behavior at all times.

The Qur'ān says:

"*You are never in a state, nor do you ever recite a verse of the Qur'ān or engage in any other action, without My being instantly aware of it. Not a single atom in the heavens and the earth is hidden from your Lord; whatever exists, whether smaller than an atom or bigger than it, is recorded in a clear book (divine knowledge)*" (10:61).

Criteria for Establishing the Worth of a Deed

Many people imagine that the worth of a deed depends on the extent of the benefits to which it gives rise. They therefore assign the highest value to a deed which appears to have greatest quantitative benefit. Such judgements of value are based on external and socially determined criteria, and the intention underlying a given act is never taken into consideration. It makes no difference whether a certain benefactor simply wishes to show off and attract the attention of society or whether he is motivated by considerations of higher order such as a pure and lofty intention.

From a social point of view, therefore, the goodness of an action depends on its benefit to society; the motive underlying it and the purpose informing it are judged immaterial.

From the divine vantage point, however, the quantitative aspect of the deed is not important at all; that which is measured to determine its acceptability to God is the quality of the deed, the nature of the inner motives that led to its performance. If someone embarks on a deed without being inspired by a spirit of truthfulness and without connection to God, the source of all being, and if his motive be hypocritical pretense and the winning of transient fame and respect, the result will be a lowering of his moral status.

Such lowly motivations strip apparently beneficial acts of all sincerity; the acts become like corpses, lifeless and valueless.

To put it differently, they are like tainted goods, quite unacceptable to God, for the author of such acts will have sold his religion in exchange for worldly considerations and will no longer deserve God's gaze of favor and compassion.

When judging the value of a deed, it is therefore totally incorrect simply to examine the degree to which it benefits society; matters cannot be judged in this pseudo-mathematical way.

A deed acquires value from the point of spiritual development only when it acquires a heavenly aspect – i.e., is oriented to the divine realm – through the flight of the spirit from the narrow cage of the instinctual self and its acquisition of pure sincerity.

Man should become so devoted and attached to God's commands that he submits to them unconditionally; his actions and deeds are done purely for God's sake, his steadfastness in obedience is for God's sake, and His reward is correspondingly with God.

It is a pure intention and aim, one in which the desire to earn God's pleasure is present, that makes man's deeds acceptable to God and enables him to earn lofty rank. The value of a deed is not then absolute, to be measured by some quantitative yardstick or in accordance with human perceptions; it is sincerity of intention that fixes its worth.

When the forces of Islam were readying themselves to

fight the enemy at the Battle of Tabuk, they needed financial support. The Prophet, peace and blessings be upon him and his family, asked some wealthy individuals to assume the costs of the battle, and each of them contributed to the Muslim army to the extent his resources permitted.

A person by the name of Abū 'Aqīl al-Anṣārī was able to earn two pounds of dates by working extra hours at night, and he offered one pound to the Prophet as his contribution. The hypocrites took advantage of the occasion to mock the Muslims by ridiculing Abū 'Aqīl's contribution. Thereupon a verse was revealed which reprimanded the hypocrites and threatened them with severe punishment in the hereafter. This is the verse:

"Those who on account of their own evil nature find fault with the contributions of obedient believers, who mock those who do not grudge spending in the way of God whatever they are able, -- God mocks them and He will punish them; a painful torment will be theirs" (9:79).

The Qur'ān also says:

"The good deeds of those who have no belief are like a mirage on a flat and waterless plain: the thirsty man imagines it to be water and he hastens towards it, but when he reaches it, he finds nothing" (24:39).

Or again:

"The deeds of those who believe not in God are like ashes that are blown away by a strong wind; no result remains for their strivings. This is misguidance, far removed from the right path" (14:18).

"Whosoever wishes to reap the fruit of his deeds in the hereafter, We will bestow on him a reward greater than the outcome of his deeds. Whosoever wishes to reap the fruit of his deeds in this world, We will permit him to enjoy it here in this world, but he shall have no share or portion in the hereafter" (42:20).

The Most Noble Messenger, peace and blessings be upon him and his family, said:

"When resurrection comes, a summons will be heard by all on the plain of gathering. The summoner will say: 'Where are those who worshipped other human beings? Rise up; go, seek your reward from those whom you desired to please with your acts. I do not accept deeds tainted by worldly intent.'"[73]

He also said:

"The value of deeds depends on the intentions underlying them."[74]

Concerning the Qur'ānic expression, "*in order that He might test you to see which of you is better in deeds*" (67:2) Imām al-Ṣādiq, upon whom be peace, said:

"What is meant here is not the extent or the quantity of deeds, but the highest degree of righteousness. Righteousness consists of the fear of God, sincerity of intention and purity of deed. To keep a deed utterly sincere and free of all contamination is more difficult than doing the deed itself. A sincere deed is one in which only God's pleasure is sought and not someone's praise. The intention is better than the deed, or is even identical with the deed, for '*Everyone acts in accordance with his own nature,*' (7:84) which means his intention"[75].

The verses and and traditions we have just cited all indicate that from the point of view of the Creator it is the spiritual state of man that determines whether his acts will be accepted or not, the same spiritual state that man is aware of in himself whenever he performs any deed. This is the criterion by which God measures and which He has communicated to mankind.

The Qur'ān says:

"*The similitude of those who spend their wealth in God's path and rejoice in God's favor is a seed sown in fertile ground; it receives abundant rain in due season and bears twice the yield that was expected*" (2:265).

The more a person's belief in God increases, the more clearly will the signs of sincere devotion become manifest in his conduct, so that the desire to earn God's pleasure comes to prevail over all other wishes.

The Qur'ān informs us that the Prophet Sulaymān (Solomon), upon whom be peace, addressed God in prayer as follows:

"*O God, inspire me to thank you for the bounties you bestowed on me and my parents, and to perform acts that are worthy of Your pleasure"* (27:19).

Yūsuf (Joseph), that sincere devotee of God, preferred the terrors of prison to rebellion against God and becoming submersed in the whirlpool of lust. Desirous of observing God's commands and preserving thereby his own purity, he prayed:

"O Creator, the pain of prison is better and more pleasant for me than the pollution of sin and rebellion against You" (12:33).

He firmly turned his back on outward freedom that would have drawn him in the direction of sin, proudly choosing a dungeon in which he would enjoy inner freedom and moral purity.

The Commander of the Faithful, 'Alī, upon whom be peace, said the following in the course of the counsel he gave to Imām al-Ḥasan, upon whom be peace: .

"Blessed and fortunate is he whose knowledge and action, friendship and enmity, seizing and loosing, speaking and remaining silent, conduct and speech, are all devoted exclusively to gaining the pleasure of God the Unique."[76]

This represents the highest ideal that might possibly be imagined.

Certain Islamic traditions regard obedience to divine command without any fear of punishment or hope of reward as the special characteristic of those who consider themselves always protected and favored by God. It is they who attain the highest degree of sincere devotion to God and knowledge of Him; they think of nothing but earning God's favor and worshipping Him in obedience. This is indeed the way in which God wishes to be worshipped.

The Commander of the Faithful, 'Alī, upon whom be peace, describes this group of men, in a profound and eloquent expression, as "free men." He says:

"Some men worship God in order to attain reward, and this is the worship of traders. Others worship Him out of fear of punishment, and this is the worship of slaves. But there are others again who worship Him out of gratitude and recognition that He is fit to be worshipped, and this is the worship of free men."[77]

Such untainted worship may also be regarded as a general and universal phenomenon, in the sense that every existent phenomenon praises and glorifies God through its implicit proclamation of the purpose for which it was created and its motion toward perfection within its own particular sphere.

Man is an inseparable part of the order of creation and is indeed its most highly developed part, and for him to separate from it would mean his collapse and destruction. He must therefore follow the universal law of nature which is the praise and glorification of God and sanctify all his relations with nature by worshipping the Creator in utter sincerity.

By orienting himself clearly and unambiguously to this aim, man is able to establish complete harmony among all the dimensions of his being and to open the gates of well-being and salvation in this world and the hereafter.

A human action can, then, be regarded as truly good and deserving of reward in the hereafter only when it arises from a pure and sacred motivation that accords with a broad and profound understanding of the universe resulting in sincere worship and an unbreakable link with the Creator. Man will then live in the shadow of God's favor and protection and be truly worthy of functioning as God's viceregent on earth.

The Commander of the Faithful, 'Alī, upon whom be peace, humbly prayed in these terms:

"I ask of you, by Your Sacred Essence and by the greatest of Your blessed names and attributes, that You adorn all the moments of my life, night and day, with the remembrance of You and cause them to pass in service and worship of You. Make my deeds worthy of Your acceptance, so that all my acts and speech are devoted to You in utter sincerity and my inward states are marked by submission to You.

"O Master, O Being upon whom all my trust is placed, and to whom my being complains of its distraught state!

"O God, O God, O God! Strengthen my limbs and members in service to You; bestow firm resolve on my heart; establish the foundations of my being on fear of You; and keep me in everlasting service at Your threshold, so that I may outstrip in devotion to You all who have preceded me; hasten toward Your presence more swiftly than the swiftest, draw nigh to You with a heart overflowing with love; and be sheltered by Your mercy together with the people of sincerity and faith."[78]

It is necessary for such utter sincerity to be continuous in order for one's acts to be acceptable to God, for it is possible at all times that righteous deeds be endangered by the effacement of their positive effects and for their authors thus to be deprived of God's reward.

Thus Imām al-Bāqir, upon whom be peace, said:

"The preservation of a righteous deed is more difficult than performing that deed in the first place." He was then asked: "What is meant by the preservation of the deed?" He answered: "Let us suppose that someone makes a gift of charity in order to earn God's pleasure and to have it recorded in his register of deeds as an act of charity unknown to men. Then he tells someone about what he has done. The reward for hidden charity is annulled for his act will have become public. He then tells someone else of what he has done, and this time sincerity with which he had performed it will be completely annulled, and he register of his deeds will record that his act was hypocritical."[79]

We should be aware, however, that the effect of a righteous deed disappears and the reward for it become annulled only when the reason for making it publicly known is hypocritical self-display, not a motive of a higher order such as encouraging emulation by others.

The aim of Islam is to create a permanent, unbreakable and all-embracing relationship between man and God, in such a way that man recognizes Him as the authority to which he should turn in all things and the commands and laws of which he should obey in every instant of his life. The presence of this firm and lasting attachment of the heart to God makes all things in life perfect and complete, and its absence reduces all things to meaninglessness and absurdity.

Can anything other than belief in God and the day of resurrection and requital impel man to act in righteousness and sincerity and to shun all forms of personal aim and motivation?

Lesson Eighteen
Testimony by the Most
Veracious of Witnesses

The Noble Qur'ān makes it clear that the testimony given by sinners in the court of divine justice will be utterly unique in nature, bearing absolutely no similarity to the juridical procedures of this world.

The verses of the Qur'ān that speak of the giving of testimony on the day of resurrection proclaim that the hands, feet and even the skin of the sinners will disclose the hidden sins that they committed during their lives and that were previously unknown to all but God; the sinner will stand revealed, to his utter dismay and terror. The animation of these witnesses and the testimony they will bear to the events that have happened in the world show that all the deeds we perform are recorded both in the external world and in the various organs and limbs of our bodies. When the conditions of this world are replaced by those of the hereafter, on the day when, as the Qur'ān puts it, *"secrets are made manifest and none will be able to conceal anything or seek help from anyone,"* (86:9-10) all the deeds that have been recorded will pour forth and begin to bear witness.

We can indeed observe in this world a pale and feeble example of what is meant by things acquiring speech.

A doctor, for example, understands the language of the body. The rate of the pulse may indicate fever, and yellowness of the eye proclaims the presence of jaundice. To give another example, we can tell the age of a tree from the circles within its trunk.

It is nonetheless true that we cannot know the exact modality of the testimony that will be given in the hereafter. However, once the veil is lifted from men's sight, their power of vision will increase and their level of perception will be raised. They will embark on a new life with enhanced means of perception and will see many things that surrounded them in this world although they were unaware of them. Thus the Qur'ān says:

"*You were in a state of negligence; now We have lifted the veil from you so that your sight is today keen*" (50:22).

Other verses speak of the multiplicity of the witnesses that will come forward:

"*Let them fear a day on which their tongues, their hands and their feets shall bear testimony against them.*" (24:24).

"*A day on which all the enemies of God will be drawn into the fire -- as they stand next to their destined abode, their ears, their eyes and the skins on their bodies shall testify to the sins they have committed. They will address their limbs in astonishment, saying, 'How do you testify concerning our deeds' They will answer, 'God who gave speech to all creatures has also given us speech. First He created you, and now He brings you back to Him. You concealed your ugly deeds not in order that your ears, eyes and skins should not give witness today, but because you imagined God unaware of what you hid from other men. It is this groundless assumption that has brought about your perdition, for today you are in the ranks of the losers*" (41:19-23).

This verse stresses that man is unable, in the last resort, to conceal the sins he has committed with his limbs. This is not because he underestimates his bodily form, which in the end turns out to have been a means for recording his deeds, but because he imagines that things are essentially autonomous and that much of what he has done will be beyond the reach of God's knowledge. It is this unawareness of the fact that nothing in creation is hidden to God that casts men into the pit of eternal wretchedness.

The Qur'ān further proclaims:

"Today We place the seal of silence on the mouths of the unbelievers and transgressors. Their hands shall speak to us, and their feet shall bear witness to what they have done" (36:65).

Imām al-Ṣādiq, upon whom be peace, said the following in clarification of this matter:

"When men are gathered together before God on the day of resurrection, everyone will be given the record of his deeds. When they see the list of their crimes and their sins, they will begin to deny them and and they will refuse to confess. Then the angels will bear witness to those sins having occurred, but still the sinners will swear that they have done none of the deeds of which they are accused. This is referred to in the verse, *'On the day when God shall resurrect them all and they will swear lyingly to God as they once swore lyingly to you'* (58: 18). It is then that God will place a seal on their tongues and cause their bodies to begin speaking about what they have done."[80]

Irrefutable Witness

Even more remarkable is the fact that the deeds man has performed will themselves take shape before his astonished eyes. This must definitely be regarded as the most veracious form of testimony possible; it closes off before the offender any defense, deception or flight from chastisement, and strips him of denial and sophistry. No crime remain unproven, and the sinners will be overtaken by shame and humiliation.

The Qur'ān says: *"On the day of resurrection they will find whatever they have done confronting them"* (18:49).

Or again:

"There will be a day on which everyone who has done a good deed will find it confronting him, and those who have done evil will wish that it were kept far distant from them. God warns you against His punishment for He is in truth compassionate toward His servants" (3:30).

Since it is impossible for deeds to disappear in the hereafter, the most that sinners can hope for is that a distance be maintained between them and their deeds, a clear expression of their disgust with what they themselves have done.

In addition to all the forgoing, and still more important than it, God describes Himself as the witness to all the deeds of men:

"Why do they not believe in the signs of God? He is a witness to all that you do" (3:98).

The Qur'ān also mentions the prophets and those who have drawn close to God as witnesses to man's deeds:

"The earth will shine with the light of its Lord. The record of men's deeds will be brought forth and the prophets and the martyrs shall be summoned to bear witness and judge among men so that none shall be wronged" (39:69).

It should be borne in mind that such witness and testimony will not be restricted to the outer aspect of men's deeds. What is meant is rather testimony to the quality of deeds with respect to their good or their evil, and whether they represented obedience or sin — in short, the inner aspect of deeds.

The giving of witness on the day of resurrection is a sign of honor and respect for those who are called upon, but it also indicates that while in this world they had a certain awareness of men's inner beings, that they were able to observe them just like their outer beings and thus to record their deeds with precision and inerrancy. It is obvious that conventional knowledge and sense perception are quite inadequate for testimony of this kind; it depends on a more profound mode of awareness that is able to embrace the inner dimensions of man, an awareness that transcends our normal capacities and permits an unfailing distinction to be made between the pure and the impure.

Such testimony is based upon a clear vision of reality, and as such it is infallible.

The Qur'ān says:

"Tell men that whatever they do God will display to them whatever they do, and the Messenger and the believers are aware of it. Then they shall return to God Who knows the hidden and the

manifest, so that they will be requited for their good and their evil" (9:105).

According to commentaries on the Qur'ān, what is meant here by "the believers" is the Inerrant Imams from the Household of the Prophet, peace and blessings be upon him and his family. They are distinguished from other Godfearing people by the special grace and favor they have received from in that they are both inwardly pure and have been utterly purified by God. It is for this reason that the giving of testimony in the hereafter has not been vouchsafed to all men of piety.

Imām al-Bāqir, peace be upon him, said in a certain tradition:

"No group or class of men can bear witness to the deeds of men except the Inerrant Imams and the prophets of God. The generality of the community has not been described by God as witnesses, because in this world there are people whose testimony cannot be trusted even for a handful of grass."[81]

* * * * *

All the deeds of men have a profound effect on their beings. If someone knows that injustice and crime are sinful but nonetheless engages in them at the behest of his instinctual nature, a contradiction will arise in his inner being that will burn and torment him profoundly. But is it not he who has created this contradiction?

If envy gnaws away at a man's inner being, is anyone responsible apart from himself?

Imām al-Ṣādiq, upon whom be peace, said:

"Sin cuts more deeply than a knife."[82]

All of our words and deeds are stored in the vast and mysterious archive of our body and our soul, and they will be brought forth in the tribunal of resurrection. The totality of our acts, good and bad, are stored up within us and will ultimately take shape to confront us.

The reckoning of men's deeds that will take place in the hereafter will, then, be utterly unique. No one may hope to obfuscate the truth or to deny the contents of the precise record that is laid before him. Everyone will be compelled to accept the truth and to submit to its consequences. The hands, the feet and the skin will be called on to give witness; God from Whose knowledge not at single atom in the heavens and earth is hidden and Who is aware of the falling of leaf from a tree, will also be a witness; and the prophets and the Imams will bear their witness to whatever we have wrought.

It is obvious that it is impossible for us now to understand and perceive fully all these dimensions of the inevitable reckoning that will follow resurrection.

Lesson Nineteen
The Assumption of Form by Our Deeds

In the past it was believed by specialists in the empirical sciences that an insurmountable barrier existed between matter and energy. Further scientific research discredited this belief so that a new theory entered scientific discourse, one to the effect that matter might be transformed into energy. The transformation of matter is accepted today as an incontrovertible truth. However, empirical science does not propound the reverse of this – the transformation of energy into matter.

Since the transformation of matter into energy has now been accepted, it is entirely conceivable that future scientific progress may come to prove the transformation of energy into matter by means of a similar process. There is indeed no proof that energy once scattered cannot be accumulated anew and take on corporeal form.

Every motion and act undertaken by man counts as a good or a bad deed, and at the same time it represents a kind of deposit in the body that is expended in the form of energy. The acts and even the speech in which a person engages are, therefore, differing forms or manifestations of energy – either auditory or mechanical energy, or, in some cases, a mixture of the two.

The fuel our bodies consume is derived, for example, from foodstuffs, and energy is released from the compounding of these foodstuffs with oxygen. This energy in turn is transformed into various kinds of motion and activity, ranging all the way from gentle speech to strenuous physical exertion.

The stability of our mental reminiscences, of our awareness of the forms which lie within the range of our knowledge, is itself an indication of the permanence of our deeds. These forms sometimes lie hidden in our minds for lengthy periods, but they can be brought forth at any moment and exercise various effects upon us, both physical and psychological.

Among the effects that may be caused by the emergence of memories are happiness and joy, sorrow and grief, the palpitation of the heart, the blushing or paling of the face, and the occurrence of disequilibrium in the glandular secretions.

It can therefore be said that our actions and words, dissolved in the atmosphere in the form of energy, are not annihilated, and that whatever we do in the course of our lifetimes is stored up in the archive of nature, an archive which the powerful hand of God has established and the permanence of which He has assured. The day will come on which nature will return to its true Owner all the trusts that have been deposited in it, and all the energies that have been accumulated in it will display themselves.

Why should the energies that have been expended for the sake of good and virtue, or evil and corruption, not take on a certain compressed form that then assumes an appropriate corporeal form on the day of resurrection? Those forms would be, respectively, unending bliss and delight and unbounded pain and torment.

We have accepted the burden of accountability and we will see the inevitable result of the way in which we have compounded our beings, in terms of both actions and thoughts, for our deeds will themselves rise up to requite us.

* * * * *

It can even be said that the very pattern of creation imposes certain effects on our acts and behavior without asking for our permission and without our even being aware of it, the result being that they grow and develop in ways we cannot suspect under our current circumstances.

With the passage of time a small seed is transformed into a great, strong tree. Similarly, various factors set to work on sperms and bring forth from them various creatures, great and small, that possess an astonishing variety.

When an alcoholic is under the effect of alcohol throughout his life he will exert a direct, undesirable long-lasting effect on his offspring.

Do not these cases furnish an analogy for the confrontation of man with the consequences of his deeds — whether punishment or reward — in the hereafter? Is it not conceivable that an act of brief duration should earn man eternal misery or eternal happiness?

Although it is difficult for us at present to grasp this matter completely, the continuous advances being make by science may help us to understand it to a certain degree.

Experts are now able to capture and record sounds from the past. Since all living beings emit a certain kind of radiation, and motion results in the creation of waves, it has become possible to measure and record the waves that are audible from centuries old pottery; it is as if the sounds made by the potter can be heard anew after several centuries. It is also possible to photograph the imprint left by the fingers of thieves at the scene of a crime, thanks to the heat of their bodies.

If all this is possible in this world, why should something similar not be possible for all our deeds in the hereafter?

The great observatories of the world can today record waves emitted by distant galaxies, thanks to the complex receivers with which they are equipped; this permits them to uncover many mysteries and secrets.

Together with the other evidence we have adduced, this permits us to suggest that from a scientific point of view the transformation of energy into matter and, therefore, the assumption of material form by our deeds does represent a tenable hypothesis.

The Non-Existence of Time

Furthermore, time is relative, being the result of the motion of the earth and the sun. If, for example, we were to travel to a certain planet, the events that take place on earth would reach the planet after the passage of a number of years determined by the distance of the planet from the earth. We would then be able to observe precisely our deeds and those or others after the passage of many years.

Similarly, certain stars that emit light and are visible to us today in fact dissolved and disappeared several centuries ago. Nothing of them remains and yet, on account of the distance that separates them from the earth, their light still reaches us on account of the distance between them and the earth.

Man's sensory powers can grasp only the surface aspect of things and are unable to grasp their inner aspects. He is therefore unaware, while in this world, of the deeds that he performs here and of the beneficial or harmful effects they will have in the hereafter. In the next life, however, whatever is hidden will become manifest, and once the book of their deeds is laid open before them, all people will see clearly the pattern their conduct has followed.

The Qur'ān, that book imbued with ultimate truth, describes the events that shall occur on the day of resurrection as follows:

"That which was previously concealed from them shall become apparent" (6:28).

The criminals who are bound in the fetters of their own lusts and desires will attempt to gain a measure of false tranquillity by hiding from themselves whatever is likely to harm them and burying the awareness of it deep within their beings. But the truth that they attempt to conceal will come forth to confront them.

The Qur'ān says:

"We have made the good and evil deeds of every individual to be a ring around his neck. On the day of resurrection We shall display the record of his deeds, and the record shall be so clear that he will be able to read all its pages at once. A summons will come to him, 'Read

yourself your own record of deeds, for it is enough that you yourself assess and measure your deeds"' (17:13-14).

Another verse reads:

"On that day man shall become aware of all the deeds, good and evil, he has committed throughout his life" (75:13).

Someone once asked Imām al-Ṣādiq, upon whom be peace, "Does man know what he will see in his record of deeds?"

The Imām replied: "God Almighty will remind him of them, so that there will be no closing of an eye, no taking of a step, no uttering a word, that he will not remember; it will be as if he had done all that the moment before."[83]

From this tradition it can be deduced that the nature of the record and of its reading will be utterly different from that of a book and its reading in this world; it will be something akin to a powerful and instant reminder.

It should also be kept in mind that the recording and registering of deeds will include both the acts that man has engaged in directly and the results and consequences of those deeds; it is the combination of all this that will be subjected to assessment and accounting. Thus the Qur'ān says:

"We shall restore life to the dead, and We record both the deeds that occurred in the past and the effects to which they gave rise" (36:12).

When in those critical moments the criminals look back at the corridors of time in which they committed their deeds they will exclaim in astonishment:

"Woe upon us! What kind of a book is this that records and enumerates with precision all of our deeds, great and small?" The verse then proceeds: *"They shall see all of their deeds, present before them, and God shall not wrong anyone"* (18:49).

"On the day that God raises up all men for the accounting to make them aware of the results of all the deeds He has recorded and they have forgotten; indeed God is a Witness to all creatures in the world" (58:6).

Corrupt friends and evil companions are at the source of much of the misguidance to which man is subject, in the realms of belief, action and morality. When therefore man recognises on the plain of resurrection those who are the cause of his misfortune, regret will engulf him and he will exclaim, according to the Qur'ān:

"*Woe upon me! Would that I had not chosen such-and-such a one as my friend, for his companionship prevented me from following God's path and led me astray*" (25:28-29).

This belated attempt at dissociation does not in any way exempt him from responsibility for the sins he has consciously committed throughout his life.

The Qur'ān depicts for us a wrongdoer who bites his hands in regret:

"*On that day the wrongdoer shall bite the back of his hand in regret and say, 'Would that I had followed the path of obedience in the world, in the company of God's Messenger!*'" (25:27).

"*Indeed, the friendship of Satan earns man perdition and misguidance*" (25:29).

They will blame Satan in order to justify themselves, but he will answer them as follows:

"*God made a true promise to you, but my promise was false. My only power over you consisted in summoning you to evil. You accepted my summons, so blame yourselves, not me*" (14:22).

It is natural that regret should be the lot of those wretches who are destined for hellfire. However, even the people of paradise are filled with sorrow when they look at the infinitely higher stations occupied by those who have drawn nigh to God; they ask themselves why they did not exert themselves more strenuously during their brief sojourn in this world, thus earning a higher station than that which they occupy.

The Most Noble Messenger, peace and blessings be upon him and his family, said:

"There is no creature that will not be overtaken by remorse and regret on the day of resurrection, but regret will be of no avail. When the blessed look upon paradise and the infinite bounties that God has prepared for the pure and the Godfearing, they will regret not having performed righteous deeds equal to theirs. As for the wretched, the people of hellfire, they will groan and lament when they see the fire and hear its roar, and they will regret not having atoned for their sins while still in the world." [84]

Two Unequal Scenes

The true worth of everything can best be appreciated by measuring it against its opposite.

The Qur'ān therefore juxtaposes the grateful joy of the people of paradise with regret of the people of hell, a regret to which is joined the impossible wish to return to the world in order to make amends. These two utterly distinct and unequal states are depicted as follows in the Qur'ān:

"*They will reside in gardens of eternity; they will be adorned with bracelets of gold and pearls, and their garments shall be of silk. They will say, 'Praise be to God Who has removed all sorrow from us: in truth our Creator is Merciful and Just in dispensing reward. Out of His bounty He has settled us in an eternal abode of bliss; no toil or weariness shall touch us therein.' The abode of the unbelievers shall be hellfire; there neither shall they die, nor shall their penalty be lightened; thus do We punish the unbelievers! They shall cry out, 'O Lord, bring us forth from here so that we might work righteousness, not that which we used to do.' They will be answered: 'Did We not give you life enough to receive admonition as others did? Did not one come to warn you? Now taste your punishment, for there is none to aid the wrongdoers*" (35:33-37).

First these verses depict the tranquil and stable abode of paradise, overflowing with blessings of both material and spiritual nature. There the Godfearing shall enjoy both the satisfaction of their material desires and spiritual peace and tranquillity. The dwellers in paradise will therefore offer thanks to God for having been guided to eternal bliss and rewarded for their deeds of righteousness. They will regard the vast realm of paradise from which all trouble and pain are absent as the result of God's generosity and favor, for they do not consider themselves worthy of it.

When we look in the other direction, we see anxiety and the terror of impending punishment engulfing the sinners. They kneel down in their misery and shame and begin to give voice to their regret in tones of despair. They wish to emerge from their fearful state in order to go back and atone for the corrupt deeds they have done.

None of this avails them, for their brief life is past and now the terrifying fire of hell burns them each second. They are not permitted to die, nor is their punishment lightened.

In short, the two contrasting scenes are of joy and tranquillity on the one hand, and misery, torment, and fruitless remorse on the other.

* * * * *

Qays b. 'Āṣim relates: "I once set out from afar with a group of companions to visit Medina. We came into the pre ence of the Most Noble Messenger, peace and blessings be upon him and his family, and I asked him to bestow some counsel upon us. I said: 'Since we are desert dwellers and only rarely come into the city, we wish to make use of this opportunity and benefit from your eloquent words.'

"The Prophet replied: 'Pride is followed by humiliation, life is followed by death, this world is followed by the hereafter. Everything that exists is without doubt subject to an accounting, and there is one who watches over all things. There is a reward for every good deed and a punishment for every evil deed. there is a set period for everything.

"'O Qays, you have a friend and companion who one day will be buried with you. When you are buried, he will still be alive although you are dead. If your companion is noble and a man of honor, he will honour you, and if he is lowly and vile, he will torment and trouble you. He will be resurrected together with you, and you will be resurrected together with him. No questions will be put to you; they will all be directed to him. Choose, then a worthy and righteous companion, for if your companion is righteous he will comfort you, but if he be wicked, you will wish to flee him in terror. That everlasting companion and friend is none other than your deeds.'" [85]

Every wrongdoer shall be resurrected with the inward countenance that he has fashioned for himself. The Qur'ān says: *"The wrongdoers shall be recognized by their countenances"* (55:4).

The Prophet, peace and blessings be upon him and his family, said:

"The two-faced hypocrite shall be resurrected with two tongues. One tongue will be at the back of his head, and the other in front. Flames shall dart forth from both of his tongues, engulfing his body. Then it will be said concerning him: 'This is the man who confronted people in world with two faces and spoke with two tongues.'"[89]

Lesson Twenty
The Eternal Nature of Punishment

The eternal nature of the punishment that the faithless and wicked are to suffer in hellfire presents a problem for many people. Given the fact that evil acts are marked by the finiteness of the world, how – they ask – can requital for those acts be eternal and everlasting? Can there be any common measure between a finite act and an infinite punishment?

A punishment that is to extend over an indefinite future does indeed represent an extreme form of torment; it is terrifying and induces a shudder merely to think of a punishment for which no limit is set in time.

It is also true that according to human judicial systems and penal provisions the punishment of lawbreakers and offenders is fixed according to the crimes they have committed; some punishments are brief in duration while others last longer. The offences men commit are not uniform, either qualitatively or quantitatively, and the penalties awarded them also cannot be uniform.

We must remind ourselves at this point that utter justice prevails in God's judging of men, for an accounting will be made of even the slightest of deeds. Neither an atom's weight of good shall remain unrewarded nor shall a single offender escape punishment, unless he benefit from God's forgiveness and mercy. How then could the punishment dispensed by God not be precisely commensurate with the offence?

If no one objects to the eternity of the paradise in which

the blessed reside, this is because paradise and hellfire are not founded on a common basis. There is a manifest difference between eternal punishment and eternal reward. The reward that God dispenses without measure derives from His generosity and mercy, and no one therefore raises any objection. The objection pertains only to faithless evildoers residing eternally in hellfire, without their torment being lessened for a single instant.

Is such a punishment for the necessarily limited and finite sin and corruption of which the sinner was guilty compatible with the principle of divine justice, even if they dominated his whole life? Let us suppose someone spends his whole life in the swamp of atheism, unbelief and corruption; it cannot last much more than a century, which is like a brief instant when compared with eternity.

In their attempt to resolve this contradiction between the justice of God and the eternity of punishment, some scholars have interpreted the word *khulūd* ("eternity") occurring in verses that deal with the punishment of sinners in the extended sense of "a period of indefinite length," thereby freeing their minds from this troublesome burden.

This interpretation is, however, unacceptable and unrealistic. Apart from the fact that it is not supported by any reliable proof, there is the general principle that we are permitted to make such interpretations only when they do not clash with the clear and obvious sense of the verse. The Qur'ān is quite clear in assigning the terrible fate of eternal punishment to a certain group of persons who in a sense have freely created it for themselves. Indeed, the Qur'ān can be said itself to refute firmly such mitigating interpretations:

"Do they not know that the punishment of whomsoever opposes God and His Messenger is the fire of hell, to reside therein eternally?" (9:63).

"They are those whose lot in the hereafter will be nothing but the fire" (11:16).

"Those who engaged in disbelief and called Our signs lies are the people of hellfire; they shall dwell in it eternally" (2:39).

"Whoever among you Muslims turns back from his religion and dies in a state of unbelief, his deeds shall vanish, both in this world and the hereafter, and he will always be a companion of the fire" (2:217).

Given the clarity of these verses, it is not possible to give them same special interpretation in order to deny the permanence of the punishment of hellfire. The text of the verses proclaims that permanent residence in hellfire shall be the lot of those unbelievers for whom all possible avenues to salvation are blocked. As for those who have committed a certain number of lessen sins and offences, they shall either spend an appropriate amount of time in hellfire or receive the kindness and forgiveness of God.

The Fear of God and its Moral Effect

It is the fear of God's just punishments that motivates many people to observe His laws, and such fear, being grounded in religious faith, has an infinitely greater effect on men's souls than coercion and force. If a person accustoms himself to shunning God's wrath. society will be protected from the sins he might otherwise have committed. Piety is, then, a powerful watchman; whenever the influence of religious teaching fades, crimes begin to increase.

Imām al-Ṣādiq, upon whom be peace, says:

"The one who knows that God sees and hears his speech and that He is aware of all his deeds, both good and bad, is restrained by this knowledge and the faith on which it rests from all kinds of sin. Such a person will fear his Lord and refuse to follow the inclinations of desire."[87]

This type of fear is quite different from those noxious fears which arise from weakness and humiliation and, far from impelling man to do anything useful, bar his path to progress and happiness. The fear that results from concern for the ultimate outcome of one's actions is like a warning to man not to pollute himself with sin but instead to embark on the path of duty and responsibility which guarantees true happiness and success. Fear of the unpleasant consequences of an harmful act transforms man into a disciplined being, one marked by caution, prudence and foresight. Such a person will perform all his tasks, great or small, with the utmost care and trustworthiness. He will reflect at all times on the greatness and magnificence of the Creator, and, suspended between hope and fear, as religion dictates, he both hopes for God's infinite favor and is heedful of the consequences of his acts, being sure not to fall into the trap of desire or arrogance.

Imām al-Ṣādiq, upon whom be peace, said:

"Fear and anxiety are like watchmen set over man's heart while hope is an intercessor on behalf of the self and its needs. Those who know God hope for His favor while they fear Him. Hope and fear are like the two wings of faith, and it is only those believers who possess both can fly toward the station of God's pleasure.

"With the eye of intellect they look upon God's exhortations and threats. The fear of God directs their attention to God's justice, which is identical with His essence, and prevents them from polluting themselves with sin. Hope in God summons them to receive His favor and generosity. In short, hope keeps the heart alive, while fear suppresses satanic inclination."[88]

Speaking of the positive effect of the awareness of death, Imām al-Ṣādiq, upon whom be peace, said on another occasion:

"The awareness of death drives away from man's inner being all lust and illicit passion; severe the roots of negligence and lack of awareness; strengthens the hope of the heart for the fulfillment of God's promises; softens and makes tender his nature, shatters the signs and emblems of idolatry; quenches the fire of greed; and displays to him the pettiness and worthlessness of the world. This is what is implied in the saying of the Most Noble Messenger: 'An hour's reflection is worth more than a year's worship.'"[89]

* * * * *

Immersion in the affairs of this world does indeed place a veil of oblivion and neglect before the vision of man; it causes him to turn his back on lofty spiritual values, so that in the end he meets death empty-handed.

One day, the Commander of the Faithful, 'Alī, upon whom be peace, entered the market of Basra. He saw people utterly absorbed in themselves and the business of buying and selling; it was as if death and resurrection would never happen. This atmosphere of negligence deeply disturbed him, so he wept and said: "O servants of the world, O slaves to the worldly! Throughout the day you are busy buying and selling, swearing oaths as you do so, and your nights are spent in sleep and a state of complete unawareness. So day and night you are unaware of the hereafter and the outcome of your affair; when, then will you prepare yourselves for the journey that awaits you, and when will you gather the provisions you need? When will you begin to remember the hereafter and resurrection?"[90]

Imām al-Sajjād, upon whom be peace, said while addressing God in prayer;

"O God, prolong my life as long as its days are spent in worship and obedience to You. If a moment should come when my life becomes the pasture of Satan, take my soul and bring my life to an end before Your dislike overtakes me or Your anger seizes me."[91]

At the same time, as long as man is in this world, he desires certain bodily pleasures and enjoyments. This urgent longing is a general one, not confined to a given group of people. The objects of this desire represent indeed a necessity, which is brought to an end only by death. Accordingly, God does not deprive anyone of these pleasures (in their pure and licit form), nor does He encourage anyone to turn away completely from the affairs of this world. However, He does encourage man to redirect his hopes away from the false and impermanent values of this world toward true values and genuine aspirations; He warns him not to be deceived by the transient and ambiguous pleasures of this world or to become so attached to his desires and longings that he is deprived of lasting reward in the hereafter. In other words, man is exhorted to devote his attention at all times to seeking the pleasure and satisfaction of God.

Acts and Punishments

Now let us see how it is possible to accept the lack of proportion that appears to be present in God's punishing the unbelievers, criminals and tyrants with an eternity in hellfire. How can such an apparent departure from justice be attributed to God?

Once we begin to look at this question with some degree of profundity, we will see that it is implicitly based on the incorrect assumption that punishments in the next world are unchanging and fixed in accordance with the legislator's assessment of the degree of the crime that is to be punished. Once this assumption is made, there is indeed no way of reconciling an eternity in hellfire with the necessarily finite nature of any offence.

However, the relationship between a deed and its punishment is a natural and ontological relationship, the latter being the fruit and result of the former; the punishment is not fixed for the deed by means of a set of fixed juridical criteria. Once this is understood, the problem can easily be resolved.

The pain and torment that the sinner suffers after resurrection are themselves properties of the deed, properties which have a natural continuation and therefore pursue the sinner in the hereafter. The Qur'ān indicates this in the following verses:

"*Their evil deeds will become apparent before them, and that which they mocked will befall them*" (45:33).

"*They will find that which they did present before them, and God shall not wrong anyone*" (18:49).

"*On the day of resurrection, men shall come forth separately from their graves to confront their deeds; all who have done an atom's weight of good shall see it, and all who have done an atom's weight of evil shall see it*" (99:6-8).

"*Whoever has done a good deed will find it before him on the day of resurrection, and likewise whatever ugly and sinful act he may have committed"* (3:30).

Imām al-Ṣādiq, upon whom be peace, said:

"Gabriel came to meet the Most Noble Messenger and said to him, 'O Muḥammad, lead your life as you wish but ultimately you will be brought face to face with death. Love whomever you wish, but ultimately the day will come when you must bid him farewell and be parted from him. Do whatever you wish while in this world, but on the day of resurrection you shall find your deeds before you again.'"[92]

What is meant by the seeing of deeds in the hereafter is man's being confronted with the shape and form his deeds have assumed in conformity to the conditions of that realm.

Despite our assumption that our deeds are the matter of an instant, lacking all permanence, they weigh so heavily in certain instances that they penetrate all dimensions of existence.

The following example may help us to understand what is meant. Imagine someone whose outlook is entirely negative and who wears at all times the spectacles of pessimism. Such a person will see the entire world shrouded in a black veil of darkness. Instead of being filled with joy or tranquillity by the wonders and subtleties of the natural realm, his spirit will be oppressed and borne down by his pessimistic mode of thought. He will never be able to remove the dark veil he has fashioned from the entrancing visage that every created phenomenon would otherwise present. This painful pessimism cannot fail to create a painful torment within his soul, giving rise there to desperation and misery. It can even be said to be more painful than blindness, for while the blind are deprived from seeing the beauteous aspect of the world, the pessimist suffers acute misery anew whenever he beholds each of the countless phenomena of creation.

From one point of view, the pessimism of such an individual can be said to be limited and finite, but since it is multiplied by all the phenomena he encounters in the world, it can also be said to be infinite: the pessimist finds himself confronted by innumerable instances of blackness, ugliness and evil.

Let us suppose that someone leads another one to the wrong path, and that the offspring of the one whom he has lead astray persist on that path. Each of the offspring then commits thousands of sins and corrupt acts. All those evil deeds will be the result of a single act the effects of which continue indefinitely; they will be like a chain going back to that first individual. All those acts will accordingly be brought back to their point of departure.

The Qur'ān says:

"*On the day of resurrection they will bear the heavy burden of their own sins, as well as that of the sins of those whose ignorance and foolishness they exploited in order to lead them astray. What an evil burden it is they will carry!*" (16:25).

Imām al-Bāqir, upon whom be peace, said:

"Whoever among God's servants established an evil custom among men will be charged with a sin equivalent to the sin of those whom he has led astray, without their sin being diminished in any way."[93]

Thus a finite action on the part of man may be equivalent to an infinite series of actions.

Not only does every human act leave some trace in the human world; its also leaves a profound imprint, of a specific type, on the world of the unseen. It sets in motion waves of attraction or repulsion; if the act be evil, the entire world of the unseen unites to repel it, and if it be good, to attract it.

* * * * *

A further error is to imagine that the relationship between an evil act and its punishment is a temporal one. The duration of punishment is commensurate with the quality or the nature of the sin, not with its duration; it is this type of commensurateness which constitutes the real relationship between our acts and requital in the hereafter. Temporal duration is not at all at issue. Once one understands punishment and requital to be the direct effects of the act itself, it is no longer logical to look for quantitative equality between act and requital.

To illustrate this point let us look at a further example. The external world manifests a kind of reaction to each of our acts; those who burn in the fire created by their deeds can be said at the same time to be suffering from the consequences of this law. Let us suppose some young man wants to fly in the air. He goes up to the roof of the building where he lives and trying to fly falls to the ground, breaking his spine and becoming paralyzed.

On account of his fantasies, the wretched youth is thus robbed of the use of his legs for the rest of his life and is condemned to pain, misery and deprivation. He indulged his fantasy for only an instant, but the consequences may be as much as fifty years spent sitting confined to his home.

This story of the fateful consequences of falling off a roof illustrates well how the results of our acts rebound upon us. Just as the home becomes a prison for the foolish young man, we also construct prisons for ourselves with our deeds. To use a different metaphor, our acts become like scars on our faces.

Is it contrary to justice that a single moment of neglect and indulgence should be followed by a lifetime of regret, that there should be such a lack of equivalence between the deed and its consequence – the irreparable destruction of life? Is there not some contradiction between the outcome of the act and the quantitative finiteness of the act itself?

Let us suppose that the person in our story were to live on not for fifty years but for several thousand years; he would still be burdened for his entire life with the consequences of that one moment's foolishness, and again it could be said that this is injust.

The connection between an offence and its punishment is therefore not a temporal one, whether in this world or the next.

Even to the penal codes that are enforced in this world, no attention is paid to the temporal or spatial quantity of the crime; it is the type of the crime, the nature of the offence, that is crucial. The number of times the crime has been committed and the period over which it has extended are not regarded as decisive.

Which should receive the greater punishment: a criminal who in one instant blows ten people to pieces by throwing a grenade at them, or someone who listens to frilovous music for ten years?

Someone may blind twenty people or more in a very short time and be sentenced to life imprisonment for doing so; is there any relationship between this offence and its punishment, in terms of duration or quantity? Of course not.

In short, the laws that are enacted among men also do not make any temporal connection between a given crime and its punishment.

* * * * *

The foregoing discussion has established that a single instance of grave crime – a murder or offence of similar type – carries within it innumerable destructive consequences, the ultimate explosion of which will cause man to burn for all eternity.

It is man himself who knowingly and willingly tramples on God's commands, who averts himself from the truth, and who pollutes himself with unbelief, atheism and sin. He creates thereby his own fate and must ineluctably suffer the consequences of his deeds.

The various examples we have cited all have one defect. The causes and reasons that lead to a given result, the way in which a foolish person is caught up in the consequences of his deeds – all this can be understood easily by people. There is nothing remarkable about such situations and they are accounted quite ordinary. By contrast, the reward and punishment that are dispensed in the hereafter are beyond the scope of our sensory experience; they are subject to doubt and may even be denied. The consequences of deeds as they become manifest in the hereafter are indeed similar to the consequences that can be seen in this world; there is, however, a great disparity in terms of scale and precision.

Our acts and conduct in this world create their own punishment and requital, which remains suspended over our head like a hailstorm until the day of resurrection. We are exclusively responsible for our own acts, because man has the power to decide freely in this life and he cannot regard himself as the mere nuts-and-bolts of society or history.

Once rebellion, corruption and disobedience engulf a person's whole being, so that he expends all his energies on wrongdoing and servitude to the basest desires, he must pay the price for his choice, which is none other than being permanently deprived of God's bounties. This entirely natural and ineluctable fate is not at all irreconcilable with God's justice, for His Essence is utterly pure of any trace of injustice.

The descent of punishment on the rebellious and sinful is nothing other than the natural result of their deeds. Likewise, what the pure and the virtuous come to enjoy is nothing other than the fruit and the effect of their deeds. Through the piety and the veracity they have practised, they have themselves produced the happiness that they enjoy both in this world and the hereafter. The truth of this is apparent from the famous saying of the Most Noble Messenger, peace and blessings be upon him and his family, "This world is the tillage of the hereafter."

This being the case, what wise person will choose the worse of the two destinies that lie open before him? Man is the shining jewel of creation; he should do nothing to detract from his brilliance by entrusting the control of his being to base desires. The burning desires of the instinctual self will find it easy to dominate completely the hearts and the wills of those who volunteer to serve them. Let us not permit the blinding smoke that arises from our desires to blind the eye of intelligence so that we stumble into the pit of eternal perdition.

* * * * *

The Prophet, peace and blessings be upon him and his family, is reported to have said:

"God Almighty will address man as follows on the day of judgement:

"'O Son of Adam! I was sick and you did not visit Me.'

Then man will reply, 'How might I visit You, seeing that You are the Creator of both worlds?' God will answer, 'Did you not know that such-and-such a servant of Mine fell sick? You did not care enough to visit him; it you had, you would have found Me with him.'

"God will then continue, 'O son of Adam! I asked you for food and you did not feed Me.' Man will reply, 'How might I feed You, seeing that You are the Creator of both worlds?' God will answer, 'Did you not know that such-and-such a servant of Mine asked you for food? You refused to feed him; if you had fed him, you would have found Me with him.'

"God will then continue, 'O son of Adam! I asked you to give Me water to drink and you refused Me.' Man will reply, 'How might I give You water to drink, seeing that Your power holds the fate of all things in its hand?' God will answer, 'A servant of Mine asked you for water to drink, but you refused him. If you had given him water, you would have found Me with him.'"[94]

The essential nature of man, in both its corporeal and spiritual dimensions, predisposes him to love and to creative effort. If certain negative impulses cause him to engage in transgression, oppression and harshness, this represents a kind of pathological state in which man has decided to fill himself with corruption and impurity; there is always a way open for him to emerge from this state.

The Qur'ān regards it as imperative for man that he should react to sin and rebellion against God with disgust. Thus it proclaims:

"*God has made faith beloved of you and adorned it to your hearts, and He has made sin and disbelief ugly and repellent*" (49:7).

In order to choose the path of justice and true happiness, to reach the shore of salvation, it is therefore enough to follow the path that our indwelling and essential nature has traced out before us.

Imām al-Ṣādiq, upon whom be peace, says the following concerning the eternal nature of punishment:

"If one group among the people of hellfire is destined to

stay there eternally, this is because it was their intention to persist in sin if they were made immortal in this world. Likewise, it the people of paradise are destined to remain there eternally, this is because it was their intention always to obey God and His commands it they were made immortal in this world. The type of eternal existence each group enjoys is therefore determined by its own aims and intentions."[95]

It is true that intention alone is not enough to earn punishment; no one can be punished merely for conceiving a certain intention. At the same time intention is like a key that unlocks the door to man's inner being and permits its contents to be seen.

Once rebellion, evil and wrongdoing reach the level in a person that he decides to sin permanently, so that disbelief engulfs his whole being, the wellsprings of virtue and good dry up within him and all paths leading to salvation and the worship of truth are blocked off.

It should be borne in mind that there is no essential contradiction between enjoying the bounties of this world and those of the hereafter; to enjoy the blessings of this world in a legitimate manner will not lead to deprivation in the hereafter.

The Qur'ān says:

"*Say, (O Messenger) 'Who has declared forbidden the beautiful gifts of God that He has created for His servants and has prohibited them from consuming clean and pure sustenance?' Say, 'These blessings are in this world for the believers, and in the hereafter there will be even purer bounties made available for them.' We set forth Our signs for a people who have knowledge*" (7:32).

Another verse says:

"*Using what God has bestowed upon you, strive to earn reward and bliss in the hereafter. Do not forget your share of this world, and do good, as far as you are able, as God has done good and been generous to you*" (28:77).

Still another verse says:

"*O God, bestow good upon in us in this world and in the hereafter, and preserve us from the torment of hellfire*" (2:200).

Islam rejects a life spent fruitlessly in abnegation of the

world, for no one is permitted to declare illicit the enjoyment of the bounties that God has declared licit.

Naturally, the life of this world must be regarded as the preliminary to the hereafter, as an occasion for earning happiness and good fortune in that realm; God has enjoined good-doing on man in order to enable him to prosper in this world and the hereafter. He further reminds him that all that has been given to him is in the nature of a trust; he should give liberally to other a share of whatever he has, in order to earn God's pleasure thereby.

One of the manifestations of God's favor is that He responds to man's exercise of liberality and generosity with the goods that are ultimately His by bestowing further reward on him.

If people are satisfied with the pleasures and phenomena of this world, God reminds them of the bounties of the hereafter, which are in no way comparable with the pleasures of this world, although they represent their continuation in more desirable form; He warns such people to lessen their attachment to the joys of this world and to aspire instead to those of the next. To miss the opportunities of this world would be to miss the rewards of the hereafter, and thus fall prey to useless regret.

The Commander of the Faithful, 'Alī, upon whom be peace, said: "How often does some vile and trivial pleasure prevent man from attaining lofty degree and bar his path to happiness!"[96]

What causes a contradiction to arise between this world and the hereafter is exclusive orientation to this world and the choice of it as ultimate goal. A hungry pursuit of this world alone will necessarily deprive man of the lofty states of the hereafter.

Man's infatuation with this world, his slavish devotion to the material joys that it offers, will inevitably alienate him from his true destiny. His intelligence will yield to lack of awareness; he will cease to advance and he will find himself stagnating at a point unworthy of his high station.

The Noble Qur'ān warns men not to make this unstable world the object of their worship and their ultimate goal, for it addresses the Noble Prophet of Islam, peace and blessings be upon him and his family, as follows:

"Turn away from those who have turned away from remembrance of Us and have no goal other than the life of this world; that is the extent of their knowledge and awareness" (53:29).

Similarly, another verse of the Qur'ān reads:

"They are content with the life of this world, but the life of this world is but slight when compared with the hereafter" (13:29).

Or again:

"They do not look forward in hope to the meeting with Us and are content with the life of this world; they are unaware of Our tokens and signs" (10:7).

Islam, then, does not devalue this world; even grants nobility to the activities of man in this world.

The fact that man's gaze should be fixed on the next world as his ideal does not mean that he should have no share of this world.

The Commander of the Faithful, 'Alī, upon whom be peace, explained the matter as follows:

"Men fall into two groups with respects to their deeds and their goals.

"The first group work and strive for the sake of this world alone, and pursue no other aim. Their immersion in material concerns prevents them from reflecting on the hereafter, because their thoughts revolve constantly around the world and its enjoyments. Their concern for the future is limited to anxiety for the state of those whom they will leave behind. They give no thought to their own destiny and the hard days that await them, and the days of their life are spent in attempting to provide for those whom they will leave behind.

"The other group have chosen the hereafter as their true aim, and all their efforts are directed to attaining that goal. The world will make itself available to them without their even seeking it, and thus they will attain both this world and the hereafter. When they rise in the morning, they will possess good repute in the eyes of their Lord, and He will grant them whatever they request."[97]

Footnotes

1. *Rāh-u-Rasm-i Zindagī*, p. 142.
2. *Ma'ānī- al-Akhbār*, p. 290.
3. Quoted in *Kayhān*, no. 8196.
4. *Khudāvandān-i Andīsha-yi Siyāsī*, Vol II, p. 75.
5. *Emile* (Persian translation), p. 547.
6. *Nahj al-Balāgha*, sermon 203.
7. *Nahj al-Balāgha*, ed. Fayḍ, Vol. IV. p. 709.
8. *Falsafa-yi Ijtimā'ī*, p. 378.
9. *Sahīfa-yi Sajjādiya*, p. 284.
10. *Khudāvandān-i Andīsha-yi Siyāsī*, Vol. I, p. 353.
11. *Mushāhadāt-i 'Ilmī*, p. 98.
12. *Jāmi' Shināsī*, p. 192.
13. *Milal-i Sharq va Yunān*, p. 167.
14. *Danistanīhā-yi Jahān-i 'Ilm*, pp. 204-205.
15. *Rūḥ al-Dīn al-Islāmī*, p. 96.
16. *Ghurar al-Ḥikam*, p. 493.
17. *Insān Maujūd-i Nāshinākhte*, pp. 102-103.
18. *'Ilm va Zindagī*, p. 410.
19. *al-Kāfī*, Vol. III, p. 251.
20. *Dū Sarchishma-yi Akhlāq va Dīn*, pp. 388-389.
21. *Rushd va Zindagī*, p. 134.
22. *Rāz-i Āfarīnish-i Insān*, pp. 180-181.
23. *Biḥār al-Anwār*, Vol. V, pt. 2, p. 182.
24. *Dū Sarchishma-yi Akhlāq va Dīn*, pp. 289-290.
25. *'Ālam-i Pas az Marg*, section 11.
26. *Ibid.*, p. 72.

27. *Usūl-i Ravānkāvi-yi Freud.*
28. *Ittilā'āt* for 23/6/43.
29. Farīd Wajdī, *Dā'irah al- Ma'ārif*, Vol. X, p. 420.
30. *'Ālam-i Pas az Marg*, p. 46.
31. *Dū Sarchishma-yi Akhlāq va Dīn*, p. 354.
32. Dr. Arānī *Khābīdan va Khāb Dīdan*, pp. 15-16.
33. *Paydāyish va Marg-i Khūrshīd*, p. 131.
34. *Mādda-yi Zamīn va Āsmān*, p. 533.
35. *Tafsīr al-Burhān*, Vol. IV, p. 85.
36. *Li'ālī al-Akhbār*, p. 456.
37. *Nahj al-Balāgha*, ed. Subhī Sālih, p. 108.
38. *Bihār al-Anwār*, Vol. VII, p. 38.
39. *Nahj al-Balāgha*, sermon 42.
40. *Nahj al-Balāgha*, ed. Fayd, sermon 164.
41. *Nahj al-Balāgha*, ed. Subhī Sālih, p. 141.
42. *Ibid*, p. 246.
43. *Kalimāt-i Qisār*, no. 227.
44. *Mustadrak al-Wasā'il*, Vol. II, p. 290.
45. *Furū' al-Kāfī*, Vol. III, p. 250.
46. *Tabarī, Ihtijāj*, Vol. II, p. 97.
47. *Khulāsa-yi Falsafī-yi Nazariya-yi Einstein*, pp. 19-20.
48. *Nahj al-Balāgha*, ed. Subhī Sālih, p. 549.
49. *Ghurar al-Hikam*, p. 757.
50. *Nahj al-Balagha*, sermon 191.
51. *al-Kāfī*, Vol. II, p. 454.
52. *Majmū'a-yi Wīrām*, Vol. II, p. 117.
53. *Wasā'il*, Vol. IV, p. 40.
54. *Ghurar al-Hikam*, p. 407.
55. *Sahīfa-yi Sajjādiya*, p. 123.
56. *Furū' al-Kāfī*, Vol. III, pp. 127-128.
57. *Bihār al-Anwār*, Vol. XIX, p. 346.
58. *al-Kāfī*, Vol. III, p. 242.
59. *al-Mahāsin*, p. 178.
60. *Ibid.*
61. *al-Kāfī*, Vol. I, p. 62.
62. *Ibid.*, Vol. II, p. 62.
63. *Li'ālī al-Akhbār*, p. 396.

64. Quoted in *Bīst Guftār*, p. 323.
65. Quoted in *Zībātarīn Shāhkārhā-yi Shi'r-i Jahān*, p. 300.
66. *Tafsīr al-Qummī*.
67. *al-Kāfī*, Vol. I, p. 66.
68. *Bihār al-Anwār*, Vol. III, p. 136.
69. *Tuhaf al-'Uqūl*, p. 483.
70. *Mishkāt al-Anwār*, p. 72.
71. *Nahj al-Balāgha*, section 133.
72. *Bihār al-Anwār*, Vol. VII, p. 252.
73. *Mishkāt al-Anwār*, p. 312.
74. *Nahj al-Faṣāha*, p. 190.
75. *Uṣūl al-Kāfī*, Vol. III, chapter "Ikhlāṣ".
76. *Tuhaf al-'Uqūl*, p. 91.
77. *Nahj al-Balāgha*, ed. Fayḍ, p. 1182.
78. *Du'ā-yi Kumayl*
79. *al-Kāfī*, Vol. II, p. 297.
80. *Tafsīr al-Qummī*, p. 552.
81. *Tafsīr al-Mīzān*, Vol. I, p. 332.
82. *Bihār al-Anwār*, Vol. LXXIII, p. 358.
83. *Tafsīr al-'Ayyāshī*, Vol. II, p. 284.
84. *Li'ālī al-Akhbār*, p. 469.
85. *al-Amālī al-Ṣadūq*, p. 3.
86. *'Iqāb al- A'māl*, p. 319.
87. *Tafsīr al-Burhān*, p. 1071.
88. *Mahajjat al-Baydā'*, Vol. VII, p. 283.
89. *Bihār al-Anwār*, Vol. III, p. 128.
90. *Safīnat al-Bihār*, Vol. I, p. 674.
91. "Du'ā-yi Makārim al-Akhlāq" in *Ṣahīfa-yi Sajjādiya*.
92. *al-Kāfī*, Vol. III, p. 255.
93. *Safīnat al-Bihār*, Vol. I, p. 665.
94. *al-Wasā'īl*, Vol. II, p. 636.
95. *Ibid.*, Vol. I, p. 36.
96. *Ghurar al-Hikam*, p. 550.
97. *Nahj al-Balāgha*, ed. 'Abduh, Vol. IV, p. 2.

Qur'ānic Index

General Index

Black-hearted ones, 37
Blasts of the trumpet,
    (*see* Trumpet)
Body,
    in *barzakh*, 176-177
    empty spaces in the, 145
    imaginal, 130
    material resurrection of
    the, 129
    reconstruction of man's, 62
    the responsible, 141
    at resurrection, 137
    revival of the original, 144
    spiritual resurrection of
    the, 130
    transformation of man's,
    60-62, 69
    transformation into
    energy, 142-146
    union of spirit and, 171
Bones, 131-134
    reassembling of decayed,
    62-64, 71
Brain, 88, 101, 103, 112, 120
Brain cells, 84-85, 87, 91,
    99-101, 103
Breed (?), James, 109
British Journal of Public Health,
    110
British scientists, 65
Burying alive, 51

C
Carrel, Dr. Alexis, 13, 73
Carrot, Dr. Philip, 110
Cells, 73-74, 91, 98, 101, 141,
    143-144

as indication of
    resurrection, 70
Chaldaeans, 51
Charcot (?), 109
Chesser, Dr. 82
Communication with the
    spirits, 105-109
Congo, 51
Corpse, 75
Creation, 33, 162
    of man, 78
    not in vain, 35
    purpose behind, 30, 32, 42
    replacement with a new, 78
    of the universe, 35
Creatures in need of God, 35

D
Day of resurrection,
    (*see* Resurrection day)
Dead, the, 51
    mourning, 158
    reviving, 70-71, 28, 133
    rising of, 127
    spirit of, 105-109, 184
    talking to, 175-176
Death, 11-19, 33, 127-128, 151,
    158, 174, 181, 219, 221
    'Alī understood, 14
    analogy of, 12
    analogy of the bathhouse,
    14
    awareness of, 218-219
    of a believer, 173
    the body after, 176
    compared to sleep, 116
    desiring, 18

* * *